London & Hertfordshire

Edited by Angela Fairbrace

First published in Great Britain in 2009 by

 Young**Writers**

Remus House
Coltsfoot Drive
Peterborough
PE2 9JX
Telephone: 01733 890066
Website: www.youngwriters.co.uk

Foreword

At Young Writers our defining aim is to promote an enjoyment of reading and writing amongst children and young adults. By giving aspiring poets the opportunity to see their work in print, their love of the written word as well as confidence in their own abilities has the chance to blossom.

Our latest competition Poetry Explorers was designed to introduce primary school children to the wonders of creative expression. They were given free reign to write on any theme and in any style, thus encouraging them to use and explore a variety of different poetic forms.

We are proud to present the resulting collection of regional anthologies which are an excellent showcase of young writing talent. With such a diverse range of entries received, the selection process was difficult yet very rewarding. From comical rhymes to poignant verses, there is plenty to entertain and inspire within these pages. We hope you agree that this collection bursting with imagination is one to treasure.

Contents

Rockmount Primary School, Upper Norwood

St John's CE Primary School, Penge

St Joseph's RC Primary School, Willesden

The Poems

Laughter

Laughter is orange
Like the sun glowing in the evenings,
It seems to laugh when it sets,
Chuckling cheerfully as it swaps with the moon.

It sounds like the roaring of a lion with its prey
A buzz of bees when they are collecting pollen,
The voices of thousands of children,
Giggling and laughing with their friends.

It feels like a fuse being lit inside you
A bounce of excitement,
When you let laughter out
Only you can stop it.

Laughter tastes like sweet sherbet tickling your tongue
It's like a spicy meal setting your throat on fire,

It smells like ash coming out of a volcano
And cookies coming out of the oven.

It reminds me of how lucky I am
To have things to laugh about.

Louise Elson (10)
Bushey Manor JM School, Watford

Anger!

Anger is red like lava exploding out of a volcano.
Anger sounds like a devil laughing and cooking people in his
fire bowl.
Anger tastes like terrible onion with its skin on being cooked for
me to eat.
Anger smells like smoke coming out of a steam train.
Anger looks like an evil man laughing his head off.
Anger feels like I'm being run over by a herd of stampeding
rhinoceroses.
Anger reminds me of how I feel when I get told off by my teacher.

Oliver Castle (9)
Bushey Manor JM School, Watford

1

Embarrassment

Embarrassment is red like me in the morning when my dad
wakes me up.
Embarrassment sounds like everybody laughing at me like
I am a baby.
Embarrassment tastes like a pickled onion slipping down my throat
As if someone is forcing it down.
Embarrassment smells like a pile of rotting onions
That have been there for a year.
Embarrassment looks like my red face with a crowd
Laughing at me.
Embarrassment reminds me of when I wet myself in public
When I was seven years old.

Bailey Richards (9)
Bushey Manor JM School, Watford

Fun

Fun is yellow like the bright shining sun,
It sounds like children laughing in the sun,
It smells like fresh fruit resting in the sun.

It reminds me of a fantastic friendship and when we were
swimming around,
It feels like I'm in a massive ball pit full of red flowers and daisies,
It looks like kids jumping up and down like mad, crazy animals,
It tastes like bright red, sparkling strawberries.

Fun is yellow like the bright shining sun,
It sounds like the children laughing in the sun,
It smells like fresh fruit resting in the sun.

Elizabeth Holland (10)
Bushey Manor JM School, Watford

Laughter

Laughter is purple like a violet balloon floating in the sky,
It feels like having a laugh with our truthful friends,
It smells like the lovely scent of perfume in the make-up shop
round the corner,
It sounds like wonderful classical music and laughter playing in
my ear
It reminds me of the amazing response a comedian gets after
their act,
It looks like the flashing red and blue lights
At the summer funfair.

Grace Ben-Nathan (9)
Bushey Manor JM School, Watford

Silence

Silence is light yellow like dry grass in the summer.
Silence sounds like nothing: it wafts around quietly.
Silence tastes like the sweetest summer fruits in a bowl
made of solid gold.
Silence smells of a soft lavender perfume drifting across the room.
Silence looks like an invisible happy face making noise loudness
stop all throughout the house.
Silence feels like soft white cotton wool on the tail of a rabbit.
Silence reminds me of reading my beautifully written book in front
of the warming fire.

Imogen Bernays (9)
Bushey Manor JM School, Watford

Hate

Hate is black like blood going down your arms
It smells like sick when somebody is sick
It tastes like Brussels sprouts when you eat them
It looks like blackness when I close my eyes.

Jack Doyle (7)
Bushey Manor JM School, Watford

3

Happiness

Happiness is yellow like the sun shining brightly.
Happiness sounds like little children laughing in the playground.
Happiness tastes like freshly baked apple pie sitting on
the windowsill.
Happiness smells like the lovely bluebells in the fields.
Happiness looks like a beautiful colourful rainbow
And the smiles of children's faces.
Happiness feels like the soft petals of a beautiful flower.
Happiness reminds me of Chessington Park.

Agne Joceryte (9)
Bushey Manor JM School, Watford

Hunger

Hunger is a like the smell of the chicken on a grill,
Hunger tastes like a juicy melon in your mouth,
Hunger sounds like people gathering around to get the taste of
hot dogs,
Hunger reminds me of the taste of bacon and warm toast,
Hunger is yellow like a desert sunny day,
Hunger feels like people eating tasty chocolate cake,
Hunger smells like bread just coming out of the baker's.

Ryan Hewett (9)
Bushey Manor JM School, Watford

Darkness

Darkness is like a skeleton sitting in its grave,
Darkness is like the taste of mud,
Darkness feels like you are alone
Darkness sounds like a shadow whispering.

Darkness reminds me of shadows whispering all around
Darkness smells like you're breathing fumes in,
Darkness looks like you are in a dark cave.

Harvey Stephenson (9)
Bushey Manor JM School, Watford

Fun

Fun is multicoloured like a firework exploding into the air.
Fun sounds like popcorn popping in the microwave.
Fun tastes like sherbet being poured onto your tongue.
Fun smells like melted chocolate being poured over
                                                sweet strawberries.
Fun looks like squiggles, swirls and stars being formed in front
                                                        of me.
Fun feels like static electricity.

Jessica Marwood (8)
Bushey Manor JM School, Watford

Fun

Fun is multicoloured like all the colours of the bright, happy rainbow.
Fun sounds like happy children playing in the large sunny park.
Fun tastes like me eating a small delicious sweet melting in
                                                my mouth.
Fun smells like the scent of a pretty flower.
Fun looks like sun swirling around the entire universe.
Fun feels like me singing on the dark gloomy moon.
Fun reminds me of my birthday when I got my lovely presents.

Elise Heffernan (8)
Bushey Manor JM School, Watford

Laughter

Laughter is yellow like my face puffing up happily with laughter.
Laughter sounds like the Joker playing a trick on the Batman.
Laughter tastes like whirlpools swirling round my tongue.
Laughter smells like fragrant fresh air on a hot summer day.
Laughter looks like a fantastic adventure.
Laughter feels like a feather inside my tummy
Tickling everything inside me.
Laughter reminds me of me and my old friend making up jokes.

Lewis Comissiong (9)
Bushey Manor JM School, Watford

Hunger

Hunger is purple like a mouldy bit of dark chocolate,
It tastes like a bitter lemon and a sour orange
It smells like a stinky stink bomb
It feels like 100 elephants trampling inside
It sounds like a pot of lava erupting
It reminds me of all those children and people in Africa
Who have no food and how they have to grow food instead of
buying it.

Hannah Wales (10)
Bushey Manor JM School, Watford

Laughter

Laughter is all bright colours, fizzing like lemonade.
It tastes like sherbet tingling and jumping on your tongue
It smells like the lovely sea salt hanging in the air
It sounds like bubbles floating away then popping with a ping
It feels like you are going to burst open like a bursting balloon
It reminds you of the fantastic times you've had in your life
It looks like a fresh rainbow glinting in the sky.

Mia Springer (10)
Bushey Manor JM School, Watford

Love

Love is pink like the sun setting on the most beautiful day,
Love looks like the first Valentine card ever sent on Earth,
Love reminds me of brightly coloured exotic flowers swaying
in the breeze,
Love sounds like clear blue waves crashing down to the sea,
Love smells like fresh-baked bread, made in an old
Victorian bakery.

Elise Voyce (9)
Bushey Manor JM School, Watford

6

Hate

Hate is black like the ashes of a hot burning fire.
Hate sounds like a howling wolf glaring at you.
Hate tastes like a rotten apple melting in your mouth.
Hate smells like an old garbage bin sitting in an alley.
Hate looks like a big ball of fluff, blowing away in the distance.
Hate feels like you're tied up in a black plastic bag.
Hate reminds me of a black hole sucking my friend up.

Sam Probert (9)
Bushey Manor JM School, Watford

Anger

Anger is as red as a huge, big fierce fire
It sounds like a very long, loud, big *crash!*
It tastes like a very bad gas smell coming in
It also smells like a bear that hasn't had a wash
Anger looks like bad stuff coming into your mouth
It feels like yucky stuff like food that's out of date and our toast.
It reminds me of being so cross with someone.

Joanna Edwards (7)
Bushey Manor JM School, Watford

Sadness

Sadness is cold like wind blowing in your face when you are lonely.
Sadness sounds like tears dripping, someone crying loudly.
Sadness tastes like sour lemons just picked from a tree.
Sadness smells like a rotten fish.
Sadness feels like cold on my face.
Sadness looks like cold ice on a frozen river.
Sadness reminds me of going to bed early.

Antony Kavanagh (9)
Bushey Manor JM School, Watford

Silence

Silence is white like there is nothing in the universe
Silence sounds like the library when it's closed in the night
Silence tastes like an apple without the juicy taste
Silence smells like a rotting leaf that fell out of the tree a year ago
Silence looks like a quiet classroom working on a story
Silence feels like the air swaying to and fro
Silence reminds me of me asleep on a Tuesday night.

Harry Clements (9)
Bushey Manor JM School, Watford

Anger

Anger is red like fireworks exploding.
Anger tastes like lava burning your tongue.
Anger sounds like a tall building collapsing and falling.
Anger smells like smoke choking your throat so you can't talk.
Anger feels like a very hot laser going through your throat.
Anger looks like big rocks exploding from the ash.
Anger reminds me of the Devil blowing fire out of control.

Michael Jalpota (9)
Bushey Manor JM School, Watford

Darkness

Darkness is black like a shadow crawling up your leg,
It reminds you of the sad and horrible things of your life,
It looks like a room with no windows or doors at night.
It sounds like a wolf howling at night.
It tastes like the horribleness of a Christmas stew
It smells like a fire with the embers cooling down.
It feels like a ghost standing next to you in the pitch-black.

Ryan James Hunter (10)
Bushey Manor JM School, Watford

Darkness

Darkness is like sneaky, slimy ghosts travelling in the Underworld,
It smells like the burnt, mouldy, smell of the sewers,
It looks like a dark shadow in the shiny, blue sky
Covering the sandy land,
It sounds like your friend telling you a scary story right in your ear,
It reminds me of the horrific stories playing on the news,
It feels like a windy breeze flowing all around you.

Hetty Rose Bostock (10)
Bushey Manor JM School, Watford

Sadness

Sadness is blue like an exploding pen full of ink.
Sadness sounds like a baby screaming its head off.
Sadness tastes like a salty teardrop.
Sadness smells like freshly peeled garlic.
Sadness looks like an innocent person getting hit by a car.
Sadness feels like a person boasting like a bully.
Sadness reminds me of when I get hurt and start to bleed red blood.

Harry Webster (8)
Bushey Manor JM School, Watford

Embarrassment

Embarrassment is red like when you are bitten all over your face.
Embarrassment sounds like the silliest song being played.
Embarrassment tastes like sour apple juice dripping down my throat.
Embarrassment smells like my dad cooking onions in the kitchen.
Embarrassment looks like a person going red in the face.
Embarrassment feels like a person hurting me badly.
Embarrassment reminds me of a devil coming to get me.

Ella Hale (8)
Bushey Manor JM School, Watford

9

Darkness

Darkness is as black as a long dead planet,
It looks like the fierce eyes of Satan,
It smells like wind in a world of rubbish,
It sounds like the breath of gods in the sky,
It tastes like a bite of a burnt out sun,
It feels sharp and cold like a heart of steel,
It reminds me of sadness and no will to live.

Alex Walsh (10)
Bushey Manor JM School, Watford

Darkness

Darkness is black like a small empty room in the night.
It smells like smoke in a choking grey cloud.
It feels like cold, cracked stone.
It sounds like the wind, whispering in the dark.
It tastes like mouldy, rotten fish.
It looks like the night sky with no moon or stars.
It reminds you of a burning log reduced to ashes by the flames.

James South (9)
Bushey Manor JM School, Watford

Fear

Fear is pale as a frightening ghost,
It sounds like bones rattling from left to right,
It tastes like lots of ice cubes being swallowed at once,
It smells like very cold water,
It looks like flour has been poured over you,
It feels extremely cold like ice down your shirt,
It reminds you of haunted houses and graveyards.

Aaron Wilson (8)
Bushey Manor JM School, Watford

Anger

Anger is red like an angry fire
It sounds like a tiger catching his prey
It tastes like a piece of last night's meat
It smells like gas
It looks like a person raging with anger
It feels like bones crashing
It reminds me of my sister getting angry.

Lauren Parfitt (8)
Bushey Manor JM School, Watford

Love

Love is pink like a princess.
Love sounds like a soft kitten purring.
Love tastes like sweets.
Love smells like perfume.
Love looks like a kiss.
Love feels like a soft, fluffy feather.
Love reminds me of my family.

Clare Reynolds (8)
Bushey Manor JM School, Watford

Anger

Anger is red like red fierce blood,
Anger sounds like a loud raging thunderstorm
Anger tastes like little people marching down your throat,
Anger smells like a burning village.
Anger looks like a sword being stuck in someone's heart,
Anger feels hot like you're on the sun,
Anger reminds me of being mean to my sisters.

Hannah Joint (7)
Bushey Manor JM School, Watford

Fear

The colour of fear is as white as a ghost
The sound of fear is a fierce high-pitched scream
Fear tastes like electric sparks all inside your body
Fear smells like a horrible chemical holding you back
Fear looks like you are a frozen statue
Fear feels like 10,000,000 ropes holding you back
Fear reminds me of haunted cemeteries.

Connor Lowden (8)
Bushey Manor JM School, Watford

Darkness

Darkness is black like a black cat in the night.
Darkness sounds like a barking wolf.
Darkness tastes like a ghost in the winter night.
Darkness smells like a red-hot burning house.
Darkness looks like a black shadow.
Darkness feels like a silky, black, long, leather belt.
Darkness reminds me of Cuffley Camp at night.

Alex Simmonds (9)
Bushey Manor JM School, Watford

Silence

Silence is as white as the fluffy clouds in the sky
It reminds me of the dark, quiet night,
It feels as soft as a pillow
It sounds as quiet as a fairy tiptoeing
It tastes as plain as flour
It smells like a pot of pink dying camellia
It looks like a very quiet world.

Natasha Devaraj (8)
Bushey Manor JM School, Watford

Darkness

Darkness is pitch-black, like a doomed world,
It feels like I'm on my own in a strange world.
It reminds me that someone has died,
It looks like a pitch-black sky with grey clouds.
It smells like nothing has happened,
It sounds like the clouds whistling away.
It tastes like a burnt spirit.

Serena Hislop (10)
Bushey Manor JM School, Watford

Anger

Anger is red like blood.
Anger sounds like lightning crashing.
Anger tastes like burning hot jolef rice.
Anger smells like smoke from burning ash.
Anger looks like the red Devil
Anger feels like hot flames.
Anger reminds me of bad things.

Archie Green-Osobu (9)
Bushey Manor JM School, Watford

Anger

Anger is red like bursting flames through your body.
Anger sounds like a massive explosion.
Anger tastes like hot ashes in your mouth.
Anger smells like a puff of choking smoke.
Anger looks like a red monster glaring at you.
Anger feels like you want to hurt someone.
Anger reminds me of the red Devil.

Obeid Hamid-Chohan (9)
Bushey Manor JM School, Watford

Hate

Hate is black like a speeding crash
It feels like you just want to attack someone
It reminds me of a lion suffocating a zebra
It smells like an old musty book
Hate tastes like a mouthful of blood
Hate sounds like an atomic bomb explosion.

Jamie Howey (8)
Bushey Manor JM School, Watford

Sadness

Sadness looks like someone crying their eyes out
It looks like rain falling from the sky
It tastes like salt from the sea
It reminds me of my dog being taken away
It sounds like a baby crying like a duck quacking
It feels like a smooth surface of a thin table.

William Rutt (8)
Bushey Manor JM School, Watford

Hate

Hate is pitch-black like a predator in distress,
It feels like you want to make someone bleed,
It sounds like a person screaming to death.
It smells like rotten eggs in the air vent.
It tastes like smelly cheese.
It looks like a gigantic roaring dinosaur.

Alexander Clarke (8)
Bushey Manor JM School, Watford

Sadness

Sadness is blue like the tears from a baby,
It looks like poor dead flowers or trees,
It reminds me of baby eggs that the mummy has left,
It sounds like the screaming of a child,
It smells like coldness in the air,
It feels like something that has failed.

Emily Whitehead (8)
Bushey Manor JM School, Watford

Anger

Anger is red like a fireman's truck,
It sounds like a thousand people shouting,
It smells like horrible smoke,
It tastes like disgusting mouldy meat,
It looks like my friend's red face when I dropped his favourite glass,
It feels like unnecessary stress.

Alex Ward (10)
Bushey Manor JM School, Watford

Love

Love is like a pink diamond tiara.
It smells like a bunch of roses in a summer garden
It feels like a fluffy heart cushion
It tastes like a cotton cloud floating in the sunny blue sky
It looks like a teddy holding onto a ring
It reminds me of hugging my mum and dad.

Molly Culverhouse (8)
Bushey Manor JM School, Watford

Fear

Fear is pitch-black like a dark cave,
It smells like crispy ash,
It sounds like a roaring tiger leaping for its prey,
It looks like a ferocious monster.
It reminds me of a monster fighting with a knight.
It feels like a scaly dragon.

Joe Baker (8)
Bushey Manor JM School, Watford

Love

Love is pink like a sweet-smelling rose.
It reminds me of a summer garden full of flowers.
It sounds like birds singing in the trees.
Love looks like a big, pink fluffy heart.
It smells like a tub full of daisies on a lovely day.
It tastes like melting chocolate in your mouth.

Naima Heath (8)
Bushey Manor JM School, Watford

Silence

Silence is white like a glistening, shiny pearl.
It tastes like the countryside air.
It looks like a clear tiny raindrop falling to the ground.
It reminds me of a bird unable to sing.
It smells like a pot full of dying roses in the dark.
It feels like a soft, fluffy cloth that's starting to turn rough.

Annalise Stockley (8)
Bushey Manor JM School, Watford

Happiness

Happiness is yellow like me and my mum
spending time with each other.
It sounds like the wind blowing gently.
It tastes like pancakes of love.
It smells like flowers falling from the sky.
It looks like love floating in the sky.

Regan Mackenzie (8)
Bushey Manor JM School, Watford

Anger

Anger is red like the sun almost exploding.
Anger sounds like a loud man shouting.
Anger tastes like rotten cheese.
Anger smells like a dustbin.
Anger looks like violet thunder
Anger reminds me of when I get told off.

Alborz Fard (9)
Bushey Manor JM School, Watford

Happiness

Happiness is green like Hemel Hempstead bus stop.
It sounds like a person tiptoeing to a railway station.
It tastes like a block of cheese.
It smells like some cheese on toast.
It looks like mash.

Rhys French (7)
Bushey Manor JM School, Watford

Hate

Hate is like someone has done something to you,
And you just hate them because they are horrible,
Hate feels like you have a devil in you
Squirting fire everywhere
It tastes like rotten eggs.

Robbie Marsh (8)
Bushey Manor JM School, Watford

Happiness

Happiness is green like a happy boy
It sounds like birds whistling
It tastes like fresh air
It smells like air freshener
It looks like a happy chicken pie.

Simeon Ben-Nathan (8)
Bushey Manor JM School, Watford

Book

B ig book or small, it's OK, buy it today
O pen the book and see it now
O K this is it, now you know it
K ind and great, they're in the library!

Lauren Smith-Hall (7)
Christ Church Primary School, Regents Park

Monsters

M onsters
O range, red or blue
N asty sometimes
S ometimes silver, red or black
T all, sometimes short
E veryone unique
R ainbow colours
S illy or strong

A re sometimes fit
R ed or teal
E scapable

S cary sometimes
C lever or thick
A re sometimes fit
R ed or blue
Y eah! *Go monsters!*

John Baker Hine (8)
Christ Church Primary School, Regents Park

Parrot Poem

Hello, I'm a colourful parrot,
I really love to talk,
I am sometimes arrogant
But rarely ever walk.

I live in the wild,
I'm sometimes mild,
Then *tweet, tweet, tweet,*
You see me taking wheat.

I make myself annoying,
By chirping really loud,
I am not good at landing,
I fly in the clouds.

Joe O'Connor (10)
Christ Church Primary School, Regents Park

The Zoo

Today I've been to the zoo,
And I had fun, others did too.
We went to have fun,
In the sun.
The gorilla pulled my hair,
And that was definitely not fair.

I saw a giraffe,
In a striped, blue scarf,
Also in the bath.

I saw a zebra,
Eating my brother's teacher Deborah.

I saw an iguana,
Having a good old chat with his friend Porana.

When I left I was so, so upset,
But when I left I shouted, 'I love the zoo so much!'

Alfie Howe (10)
Christ Church Primary School, Regents Park

Happiness

It sounds like a butterfly fluttering in a field,
It tastes like a sweet strawberry in my mouth,
It smells like a chunk of candyfloss in a funfair,
It looks like a field of flowers, all different colours,
It feels like having a massage in a salon,
It reminds me of my family getting together.

It sounds like a bird tweeting in a tree,
It tastes like a fruit salad, juicy in fact,
It smells like a rosy red rose, growing in a garden,
It looks like a lion cub hugging its mother,
It feels like a breeze on a hot sunny day,
It reminds me of being with my best friends.

Caitlin Nicholls (10)
Christ Church Primary School, Regents Park

Birds

Birds will fly,
Up to the sky,
Eventually they will die,
But they don't lie.

A squeak from a hawk,
A twitter form a tweety bird,
But have you seen them eat lemon curd?

Penguins swim,
As they are slim,
They wear a black and white coat,
And they stay away from the boat.

Birds have a certain height metre,
They star in Blue Peter,
They twitter and make a lot of litter,
And sometimes they jitter.

Karam Ali (10)
Christ Church Primary School, Regents Park

Rain

Rain can cause me a lot of pain,
When you want to chain it, it seems to unchain itself,
Rain runs down the lane in autumn, spring, summer and winter.
Rain is one of the most common things in the world.
It's faster than a train and sometimes, in some countries,
Rain is stronger than a crane.
Surely everyone would wish they could tame rain.

R for runaway
A for annoying
I for ignore
N for a net to catch the rain.

Zana Biblekaj (8)
Christ Church Primary School, Regents Park

The Odd Zoo

I went to the zoo
The monkey ate a shoe
So did the donkey
The lion was boring
But the cubs were adoring
The parrot was biting
While the bears were fighting
The giraffe was sad
And the hippo was bad
But the bugs were the best,
Then I just left.

Harry Sims (10)
Christ Church Primary School, Regents Park

The Train

There once was a girl called Jane
Who was always in pain
She got on a train
And it led her to Spain
She always had a stain on her clothes
Below her sink there was a drain
She met a professional wrestler named Wayne,
And she went to live on a lane
She was also insane
So that's why her name was Jane!

Nayha Romero-Pinto (7)
Christ Church Primary School, Regents Park

Blue!

Blue makes me go to the loo
Blue is as bright as glue
Blue is the colour of goo
When it gets on my head it gives me my clues
I get the flu and I drop my shoe.

B for bright
L for light
U for unique
E for elegant ball gowns.

Sara Shafique (7)
Christ Church Primary School, Regents Park

Darkness

Darkness is scary,
Mean and dangerous
Darkness is very fearful
Horrible and disgusting
You hide under your covers,
When the lights go out.

Skeletons popping out of your door
Oh no! there is more.
I'm so *scared,* I have wet my bed!

Eleanor Johnston (9)
Christ Church Primary School, Regents Park

Ballet Dancers

All the dancers glance and dance in joy
The dancers put their soft shoes in the loft
And make sure their little pink dresses don't shrink in the wash
We hope your dog doesn't bite your light white dress
Dancers dance in the night which is alright.

Aleena Paracha (8)
Christ Church Primary School, Regents Park

23

Pop!

There is a drink called Fizzy
It makes people dizzy
And when it pops
It makes you hop
Now that's a nightmare sizzy!
So when you re in bed
Don't look out for scary Ted
Or he'll jump up eat a cup
And get the med.

Anjum Tasshin Hossain (7)
Christ Church Primary School, Regents Park

Football

F rank Lampard said, 'Chelsea had their best season
    at Stamford Bridge.'
O range is Reading's away kit
O range is Plymouth's away kit
T ottenham's next game is Liverpool at Anfield
B lue is Chelsea's home kit
A ston Villa are going to play against Derby next season
L iverpool are second in the table
L eyton Orient are still staying in League One!

Jack White (8)
Christ Church Primary School, Regents Park

Football!

Man U are the best,
Cos they are the best,
And that's why Man U rule.

Liverpool are the worst,
Cos they are the worst,
And that's why Liverpool drool.

Alvi Rashid (10)
Christ Church Primary School, Regents Park

24

Fred The Budgie

There once was a budgie called Fred,
Who balanced a plate on his head,
He ate some cheese,
And fell on his knees,
He went on the bus,
Without a fuss,
To buy some seeds,
For his needs,
There once was a budgie called Fred.

Ashleigh Greenaway (10)
Christ Church Primary School, Regents Park

Trip To The Zoo

Tigers are stripy
Cheetahs are spotty
Lions have a mane
When sharks bite you it's a pain
Monkeys are silly
The zookeeper's name is Billy
Spiders are scary
Bears are hairy,
The zoo.

Rayhan Hoque (10)
Christ Church Primary School, Regents Park

Cars

My friend eats spaghetti
In his fat Bugatti
He has cool wheels,
From really good deals,
He drives like a dog,
In the misty fog.

Akheem Ahmed (9)
Christ Church Primary School, Regents Park

25

Different Friends

Bella the ballerina,
Have you seen her?
Her tutu is so bright-ful,
Her shows are so delightful
Her friend is named Heather,
She controls the weather.
The pair are together,
They'll be different friends forever!

Fernanda Smith (8)
Christ Church Primary School, Regents Park

Travelling Round And Round!

Travelling round the world,
Up, down and all around,
Different transport,
Aeroplanes, trains, cars and boats
Lots of fun
Hot countries, cold countries
Spicy food, cold food
I want to travel more.

Miryam Himri (9)
Christ Church Primary School, Regents Park

Rainbows

Some people say the rainbow's wonderful
Others say it's very colourful
Look at the red, see it in your head
Look at the blue, it's the sea or goo
Look at the yellow, your best fellow
Look at the pink, it's all you can think
The rainbow will flow and now you know . . .
How high you'll fly.

Abel Ayettey (8)
Christ Church Primary School, Regents Park

Colours

Colours everywhere
There's pink and blue and lots, lots, lots more
There's colour in flowers
There's colours in paint
There's colours on books
The colours of the rainbow are
Red, pink, orange, purple, yellow, blue, green, violet, indigo
They're the lovely colours of the rainbow.

Phoebe Millard (9)
Christ Church Primary School, Regents Park

Colours Every day

On Monday the sky was white,
On Tuesday the sky was green,
On Wednesday the sky was pink,
On Thursday the sky was blue,
On Friday the sky was red,
On Saturday the sky was yellow,
On Sunday the sky was orange.

Sharmin Rahman (10)
Christ Church Primary School, Regents Park

Chelsea FC

My name is Daniel
I support Chelsea too,
I want to play for them when I'm 22,
My hero is Lampard and Terry too,
Our manager is Guus Hiddink,
Come on Chelsea, let's keep winning!

Daniel Horn-Marquez (9)
Christ Church Primary School, Regents Park

Wonderful World

The world is really cold but also it swirls
Helping each other to swirl around and around,
You should watch out, I'm coming around and around
With clothes and with little blue boxes.
What a good thing to do.
I want to help you, trust me and my swirl world.

Jaimee Bossert (8)
Christ Church Primary School, Regents Park

Louise

There once was a girl called Louise
Who really, really loved cheese
She ate it all the time
Then she was fine
But she hated saying please!

Aimee O'Connor (10)
Christ Church Primary School, Regents Park

Spy

There was a young spy,
Who loved eating chicken pie
And always looked up at the sky
And couldn't stop to have a little bit of a cry
So he always had to tell a lie!

Verona Alili (8)
Christ Church Primary School, Regents Park

Ball

B alls can roll and you have to kick them
A ll balls are different colours,
L et's play football on the football pitch
L ots of footballs are different sizes.

Sana Nasser (7)
Christ Church Primary School, Regents Park

Do Not Read This!

'What's that?' said Jack,
As he saw something on the shelf.
'Does that sign say
This will damage my health?'
He took the book from upon the shelf
And heard somebody speak
It gave him such a shock
He felt his legs go weak
Jack turned and ran, with wobbly legs
He wanted to run and run
The evil voice whispered menacingly,
'I'll get another one!'

You!

Bailey Barringer (9)
Ealdham Primary School, Eltham

Khamari

K angaroos go hop, hop, hop
H opping along all day
A ustralia is where they're from
M other kangaroos have a pouch for the baby
A ll they do is hop all day
R esting all day, hopping all night
I love kangaroos, as they hop, hop, hop.

Khamari Allen (7)
Ealdham Primary School, Eltham

Writing Club

W riting club is really fun
R eading things that we have written
I love writing club!
T hursday is our special day
I t's the best day of the week
N ever miss my favourite club
G ot to win this competition!

C ommas, full stops, question marks
L earning new things every week
U p-and-coming authors
B rilliant fun!

Jareda Cudjoe (7)
Ealdham Primary School, Eltham

Wally

Wally's such a wally,
He forgets to pay for his trolley
What a wally!

He has a brother Ollie,
He stole his sister's dolly
Ollie's a wally!

The rain poured down and soaked poor Molly,
She forgot to take her brolly
What a wally!

Johnathan Turner (8)
Ealdham Primary School, Eltham

The Bee

Sleeping for hours
In a pile of flowers
I saw a huge bee
Coming towards me
Then it stung me, viciously
Flying back to the honey tree
Oh I'm so sorry my brother bee
How about you have some tea!

Anna Cotton (10)
Ealdham Primary School, Eltham

My Week

Monday is a normal day
For playing my games
My mum has finished work
As I start my homework.

Tuesday is a different day
As we play, play, play
In football training
As it starts raining.

Wednesday I go to school
As school ends it gets cool
I go to steel pans
And they go *bang bang bang*.

Thursday is the worst day
As I get bored, bored, bored
We get no reward
Can't wait to go home.

Friday is the best day
For having fun
Now it's the weekend
So we run, run, run.

Keisha Morris-Cumberbatch (9)
Kenmont Primary School, Harlesden

My Normal Day

8 o'clock, got to get up!
Quickly eat, 'Mum, I need a cup!'
Brush my teeth, wash my face
Get dressed, do my shoes, now to tie my lace
Finally I get to school, not too late
Here comes Maggie, my mate!

Play around have some fun!
Running around in the sun
Yes! here my teacher comes
She's as sweet as honey
And as ripe as plums.

Now we go upstairs, time for work
Now it's about germs and dirt
Now it's maths - the best
Because I always come first in my test!

Now for break, but it's cold
When I go outside my arms feel all old
I don't like it out here, I wanna be inside
I wanna be where you don't have a frosted side.

Time for lunch, yum, yum, yum!
All this food goes in my tum
I want seconds, thirds, fourths and eighths
I didn't care how much I got, I just ate, ate, ate
I've eaten too much, my stomach hurts
It feels like it's going to pop and squirt.

Assembly's no fun, cold and boring,
Soon everyone in my class starts snoring,
Assembly's nearly over, five minutes to go,
Oh no! the clock is going slow
Finally it's over, hip hip hooray
Now it's the end of the day!

Well that's my normal day, I don't know about you
Well I've got to go home now
So bye, see you soon!

Maya Adjei-Van Dyke (10)
Kenmont Primary School, Harlesden

Under The Sea

Hear the water lap
Upon the golden shore
No one really knows
That under the sea there is more

In the ocean right down under
There are creatures
That swim like thunder
And creatures as big as Spain
With stings that would put you in so much pain

There are creatures as bright as the sun
And creatures that eat you for fun
And all sorts of things
That would give you such a scare.

But what I haven't told you
Is that this is my imaginary world
So come and join me for a twirl
If you sometimes want to play
Come and join me any day.

Esme Moser (10)
Kenmont Primary School, Harlesden

Friendship

F riendship is important
R espect others
I nclude others
E ncourage others
N ew people should be treated nicely
D on't ruin your friendship
S upport other people's designs
H elp other people
I ndigo is the colour of our group
P eople should be treated with respect.

Portia Buncombe (9)
Kenmont Primary School, Harlesden

Football Frenzy

On the way to the match I'm full of excitement
The car's tyre goes flat, time for a patch
I have a feeling I just can't fight it.

At the match we could be late
Hurry up, I can't wait
Mum, my team is on, come on, let's get to our seats
I don't want to miss kick off.

Oh Man United's got the ball
It's Rooney and Ronaldo going for goal
But it hits the pole
Here comes Tevez, he takes a shot and it's the pot
Right at the back of the net, goal, goal goal.

That was fun, can we go home so I can listen to Flo' Rider
Mum, thanks for that, now we can go to Auntie Pat's.

Tareek Frater-Simpson (10)
Kenmont Primary School, Harlesden

The La La Mackalok

The La La Mackalok
Is a mythical creature
It has some very interesting features.

It sits and sits in my garden all day
Until I tell it to go away.

It plays with the weeds and the vegetable patch
And all it does is scratch and scratch.

It's purple with some orange spots
It has some hair,
It's everywhere.

I like the La La Mackalok
I like it
A lot!

Maggie Mae Innes (9)
Kenmont Primary School, Harlesden

34

Water

Hear the water go drip-drop
Like a fish dropping in the water
What a world of sprinkling blue sea
Near a very big fat tree
The sprinkle, sprinkle in the blue sea.

Hear the whoosh in the shower
Make sure it's not on full power
The sea goes *splash* going side to side
Like a wave but it doesn't fly from side to side.

Hear the bath go *splish splash* in one dash
If you want you can get in, in a flash.

Hear the sea next to a tree going 1, 2, 3
I want to see the waves splash in a dash.

Lauren Heywood (10)
Kenmont Primary School, Harlesden

On The Road!

On the road people shout, shout, shout,
Cars go *vroom, vroom, vroom*
And babies cry, cry, cry.

Up in a house I hear a shout and a cry
But no one is there to make it right
'Hey you,' I hear.

So I walk some more
Then I step on a mouse
And it goes *squeak, squeak, squeak,*
But a boy called Clouse says,
'Get off that mouse.'

I see a horse doing its course,
It does not have a choice.

Loquesha Taylor Roberts (10)
Kenmont Primary School, Harlesden

The Jungle

In the jungle there are monkeys swinging up and down
Rhinos running all around
Hippos swimming in the pool,
And zebras by the tree using the loo.

In the jungle you will find that baby animals are maybe blind
If you ever go to the jungle
The monkeys will want to fight with delight
They will drop fruit on your head
So when they jump down just knock them dead.

Kieran King (9)
Kenmont Primary School, Harlesden

At Home

Wah goes the baby
Bang goes the drum
Dada goes the sax
And so does the trombone

The burning of the food
The beeping of the smoke alarm
The fight of the boys
And the running water in the bath.

Ahmed Ahmed (9)
Kenmont Primary School, Harlesden

School

When I go to school I feel cool
When I go to training I take the train
When I take scissors I cut my finger
When I take the ball I kick it around my room.

Danilo Columbo Cruz (10)
Kenmont Primary School, Harlesden

On The football Pitch

On the football pitch the whistle goes for kick off
Don't be late, do your job, do it right or get the sack
I am running down the wing

The ball at my feet, the other team feel my heat
The other team sweating
I'm not, just watch me,
Now the goal moves . . .
Celebration, *'Heter reter yo hater yes!'*

Kyle Clement Annon (9)
Kenmont Primary School, Harlesden

Kenmont

Kenmont is the best of all
Pupil of the week is all about good
If you're not good I think you should
Mr Gitten is a good TA
Come to his class, you get all the help in every single way.

If you think we have bad children in this school think again,
The children may be bad but they will always try their best.

Devante McLeish (10)
Kenmont Primary School, Harlesden

Jaws

I am the shark and I eat little fish
Sometimes I hunt very fast and I jump out of the sea
I swim to the dark deep water, don't come after me
I am very good at hunting, I'm very fast
I'm a great white, I am Jaws!
Raahhh!

Miles Hughes (10)
Kingsgate Primary School, Kilburn

Captain Jack
(Inspired by 'The Highwayman' by Alfred Noyes)

The storm was a tiger roaring,
The thunder was crashing,
Crashing, crashing
Across the lonely seas.

He came across the shivering sea,
He sailed across the ocean
Sailing, sailing,
With his blood-red boots up to his thighs.

Jack saw the mermaid Lilly
The beautiful golden mermaid Lilly - swimming,
Swimming, swimming,
Side to side like a fish in the lonely sea.

She sat on her hard rock
He kissed her lips and said,
'Watch me by sunset -
Sunset, sunset.'

He sailed away to get some gold
The Queen's men saw him there
His eyes went hollow with angriness,
Angriness, angriness.

Lilly looked out of the amazing sea
She never saw them come sailing
Across the lonely sea,
Lonely sea, lonely sea.

They tied her to a sharp shark
Until she saw Jack coming.
She killed herself to save him
Her blood was dripping
Dripping, dripping.

Nasima Begum (10)
Kingsgate Primary School, Kilburn

38

Captain Peter
(Inspired by 'The Highwayman' by Alfred Noyes)

The moon was flickering reflections
The sea was a blanket of fog
The air a mist of darkness
The grand mystical ship came
Sailing, sailing, sailing.

Towards the Island of Skull
Captain Peter was a fearless pirate
Wearing a black eye patch
A long garment of gold
And boots up to his thigh.

He reached the island and who would be waiting there
But the chief's brown-eyed daughter
Rebecca was wearing a gold dress
Peter said, 'Look for me by the moonlight
I'll be going for gold'
Tom the messenger heard and he told King George's men.

They came marching, marching and marching
They said no word to the chief, they drank his ale instead
They used Rebecca as bait
'Now watch for your love,' they said
She waited for the footsteps of the horse
As she heard the sound of the hooves
Rebecca got ready for her plan
The time came closer and closer
And then *bang* went a big loud noise.

Peter went back the way he came from
As he didn't know it was her
Till the morning came and he heard
Then he was killed.

Samiha Azam (10)
Kingsgate Primary School, Kilburn

The Pirate
(Inspired by 'The Highwayman' by Alfred Noyes)

The sun was a scorching flame
The sea was a shivering cockroach
Whistling, whistling, whistling
Towards the lonely sea.

Captain George came sailing
With his brave, fierce men
Sailing, sailing, sailing
Towards the deserted island.

The brave pirates met Amy
And the golden-eyed mermaid came
Swimming, swimming, swimming
Across the frosty sea.

'Watch for me by sunset
I'll come to you by sunset,'
Sunset, sunset
Whenever you'd love me to.

Amy was bored,
Amy was waiting,
Yawing, waiting,
Until Queen Elizabeth's pirates came.
The pirates kidnapped her
And tied a sword to her neck,
Shouting, shouting, shouting
So she could not mumble or scream.

Amy's heart pounded with shock,
Amy's veins pounded with shock,
Pounding, pounding, pounding,
All around her.

Gjenis Kajashi (9)
Kingsgate Primary School, Kilburn

Lauren And Captain Harold
(Inspired by 'The Highwayman' by Alfred Noyes)

The moon was shining above the sea
Reflecting a wonderful reflection
The waves were going mad
Here, there, all over the site
The sea was a freezing ice cube
That you couldn't even put a finger in.

Then Captain Harold came sailing,
Sailing, sailing, sailing,
He was a fearless man
Never to be frightened
And his true love was Lauren
With her long fair hair.

Dobby, the crazy man, listened,
He heard the captain say,
'I'll find some gold and diamonds
 But I'll be back soon.'

Lauren didn't know who stood behind
And the navy crew were there
They made her walk the plank
But no, she didn't jump,
Jump, jump.

She saw her captain's boat
So she jumped and saved his life.

It was in the morning he found out
It was Lauren who jumped.
Chop! Chop! Chop!
His head was chopped off
And they kicked his body in the water.

Taylor Cunningham (10)
Kingsgate Primary School, Kilburn

The Storm

The storm was a rhino with vicious rage
The thunder was a crash of lightning
It crashed, crashed, crashed
Across the lonely seas.

He came by the centre of the shivering seas
He sailed across the lonely seas,
Sailing, sailing, sailing,
With his deadly looking boots up to his chin.

The pirate spotted the mermaid with his vicious eyes
The golden-haired mermaid!
Swimming, swimming, swimming,
As quick as an octopus.

As the clouds were shivering with anger
The gusty wind blew the ship apart.
Shivering, shivering, shivering,
It as like a tornado throwing the ship away.

Soon he could see the soldiers
Coming towards his way
Thunderously he turned the ship around
Turning, turning, turning.

But it was too late,
They came too fast and furiously
And grabbed the mermaid's silky tail.

The soldiers could see a tail pointing
They grabbed it and got the mermaid.
They demolished the pirate's ship
And the mermaid . . .

Orland Galjani (9)
Kingsgate Primary School, Kilburn

Sarah And Captain Jackson
(Inspired by 'The Highwayman' by Alfred Noyes)

The sky was like a misty star
As it gently travelled over the sea.
The waves were being horrendous
Squishing your feet through the sand.
The moon was a shimmering flower
Spying your every move.

Then Captain Jackson came
Sailing, sailing, sailing.
He was fearless,
A famous robber and he loved his beautiful Sarah,
Sarah with her long silky brown hair.

Chip, the deck cleaner, overheard
Captain Jackson say to Sarah,
'Wait for me by moonlight,
I'll bring some gold by moonlight.'

Sarah never noticed who stood behind her.
Five navy men stood up straight.
They made her walk the plank, she never
Jumped, jumped, jumped.
She saw her love riding in a little blue boat,
So she jumped and saved his life.

It was early morning before he found out who'd jumped.
It was Sarah, who'd died.
So he ran, ran, ran.
On his way he got sliced, sliced, sliced,
And there went Captain Jackson,
Dead as a crabstick.

Mariana Augusto (10)
Kingsgate Primary School, Kilburn

Captain Sheanton
(Inspired by 'The Highwayman' by Alfred Noyes)

The sun was a scorching flame,
The clouds were dark as coal.
The wind travelled, travelled, travelled across the frosty seas.
Along came sailing, sailing, sailing,
Captain Sheanton looking for his beautiful mermaid
On golden rock, her name was Elizabeth.

Over the frosty seas there was a land
Somewhere hidden, unknown, where
The golden sparkly rock was, with the mermaid. So Captain
Sheanton went
Searching, searching, searching on his ship.

Captain Sheanton found Elizabeth
The beautiful mermaid. 'I will
Bring you back some gold, I
Will be back in moonlight.'
Then the mermaid replied, 'I'll wait here and we
Will run away together.' Tim the oyster
Was listening, he was in love with Elizabeth too.

But as soon as Tim the oyster heard
That Elizabeth agreed with him, Tim the oyster
Pushed her off the rock and she hit her head,
She died and fell into the deep ocean.
Captain Sheanton heard the water splash and rode back and killed
Tim the oyster,
Then he walked over to Elizabeth and cried on her shoulder.

Sally Badawy (10)
Kingsgate Primary School, Kilburn

Pirate Jack And The Mermaid
(Inspired by 'The Highwayman' by Alfred Noyes)

The moon was a ghostly light
The cold wind was a ball of air
Blowing, blowing, blowing
Across the lonely sea.

Pirate Jack was sailing
Towards the deadly island.
He found a mermaid alone
With long black shiny hair.

He called her to look at him
Her name was Lisa Michel
Pirate Jack said to her,
'Watch me by moonlight and be safe
Watch me, watch me, watch me.'

Pirate Jack gave her a kiss
He went off to the lonely sea
Lisa was watching Pirate Jack
Suddenly somebody got Lisa, Lisa, Lisa.

When Lisa opened her eyes
She saw some soldiers
She was tied to a hard pole
The soldier shot Lisa with
Dark red blood going down
Pirate Jack came back, back, back

Majid Ahmed (10)
Kingsgate Primary School, Kilburn

Prince Jake
(Inspired by 'The Highwayman' by Alfred Noyes)

The sea was a magical potion
To make people happy
The moon was a reflection
From the sea.
Across the sea Prince Jake
Came riding, riding, riding,
The prince came to SunShore City.

He came with his M11 boat
Albal was the most beautiful woman
In SunShore City.

Albal ran back to the
Huge lighthouse
As she stepped up the lighthouse
She heard a giggle then *bang!*
King George's men captured her
But unluckily Prince Jake came
He was at the door.

Albal got a different gun
And shot herself
To warn him but
He crashed through the door like a madman
But unfortunately he got shot.

Mërgim Peci (10)
Kingsgate Primary School, Kilburn

The Merman
(Inspired by 'The Highwayman' by Alfred Noyes)

The sun was setting down the foggy sea
With specks of white shining indecently.

The merman came swimming, swimming and swimming
Up to shore near Crystal island.
But why? To meet the beautiful Princess Lylica.
He wanted to marry sooo much
But it would have never worked because
The merman was half fish and Lylica wasn't.

When he reached the shore there he saw Lylica with
Long blonde hair and red glittery lips that shone upon the sea.

But the merman never realised that John the Oyster
Was watching like a dumb bulldog.
And as he watched, he overheard the merman say,
'Watch for me by moonlight near the crashing sea.'

John was furious to hear that
So he called King Draguler to put Lylica on the bay, so he did.
But Lylica realised what he was going to do so she killed herself
Not knowing the merman was watching.
So he went up to them and they killed him.
One stormy night, the merman started dancing, dancing, dancing
On the sea with Princess Lylica.

Arona Qosaj (10)
Kingsgate Primary School, Kilburn

The Young Pirate
(Inspired by 'The Highwayman' by Alfred Noyes)

As the storm began to head north
The young pirate battled the terrifying ooao
Crash, crash, crash
Just to see the beautiful mermaid.

He whispered, 'I'll battle tonight to see you.'
She looked for him at noon
But he died not appear,
Appear, appear, appear.

All of a sudden
Out of nowhere he came.
It was the evil hook-man pirate
Hook was an ugly, spotty fiend.

He dragged the mermaid out of the water
And she shrivelled up and died
On the golden bank.

The next day he found the mermaid dead
Laying on the bank.
He ran for the murderers,
Dead, dead, dead.

He had nobody to care for, he shot himself dead.

Ellie-Marie Buxton (10)
Kingsgate Primary School, Kilburn

Captain Skull
(Inspired by 'The Highwayman' by Alfred Noyes)

The moon was a glowing ball,
The waves were slithering snakes,
The sky was a dark hand
Crawling towards the moon.
The enormous ancient ship came,
Sailing, sailing, sailing
To the beautiful island.

Captain Skull was wearing a
Crooked red pirate hat, ragged shirt and baggy trousers.
He arrived at the beautiful island
To see Emily the wealthy landlord's daughter.
She had gorgeous brown eyes and lips as red as roses.
She was sitting under a tree tying her hair in a plait.
Captain Skull told Emily he would be back at moonlight carrying a
bag of gold.

Pirate Tom was listening to the conversation.
Pirate Tom's men took Emily to the ship and put her as bait for
Captain Skull.
Emily wanted to save Captain Skull so she jumped off the ship and
drowned.
Captain Skull shot himself because Emily died.

Dania Othman (10)
Kingsgate Primary School, Kilburn

I'm The Sea

I am the sea
I am the power of thee
You can swim around me.
My colour is blue
And now you have a clue.

Ships go sailing, sailing, sailing
Above me.
I am sparkly as the jewelled sky
I am the sea.

Water's in my soul
And I'm not letting go.
My tides crash like a lion
Jumping on its prey.
Fishes and mammals, I carry them all.
My colour is a wonder and all that's under.
Fishes under me are the rainbow
But the main part is that
I am the sea.

Laiba Kamal (10)
Kingsgate Primary School, Kilburn

I Am The Sea

I am the sea, crashing and wailing
I am the waves, swirling and falling
I am the sand, as still as can be
Because I am the sea.
With sharks in it, eating and defeating,
With dolphins hiding and whining
And stormy nights and great days.
I can play with you and kill you
I keep you cold and I split countries up
And I let oil rigs go in-between me
Because I am the sea, the dark, dark sea.

Chloe Fair (9)
Kingsgate Primary School, Kilburn

I Am The Sea

I am the sea
You can swim around me.
I am blue and grey.
I am the sea
Everybody loves me.
My colour is a wonder.
I am the sea
The ships swim above me.
I am liquid.
You can hear me
Howling day and night.
I am the sea.
I am always awake.
I am as wide as the sky.
I am the sea
And you can be the sea too.

Eliya Mattis Jama (10)
Kingsgate Primary School, Kilburn

The Sea

I am the sea that crashes on the golden shore.
I am the wild sea that gallops like white horses.
On cold days I am shaking but on hot days I'm baking.
I am older than World War I and I'm older than dinosaurs.
I was actually the first thing in the world.
I am the sea that starts the waves,
When I'm angry people hide in caves.
So as you can see, I'm sometimes a swarm of bees.
When it is nap time I am the only one awake.
So this is my life as the sea,
It's lonely without a friend
Splashing, splashing, splashing forever.

Sanjeeda Ahmed (9)
Kingsgate Primary School, Kilburn

I Am The Sea

I am the sea, the blue, dangerous, wild sea.
My crashing waves are like a desert
My waves are as golden as a coin.
I'm as fast as your mind.

I'm as deep as your memory
I am the sea, I twinkle like a star.
My waves are as big as you,
The murderous ship is as gigantic as a building.

I am the sea; my waves are as strong as a Minotaur.
I am a slimy customer
My waves crash onto the ship like deathly hounds chasing you.

Gentrit Krasniqi (10)
Kingsgate Primary School, Kilburn

My Moody Teacher

My moody teacher
Is moody on Mondays.
She makes me do lots of work.
I get more than everyone else
Because she thinks I am smart.

I give it to the boy behind me
Because he is smarter that me.
Then all of a sudden I shout out
'Mrs Moody Pants, I am a liar!'

She says 'What do you mean you're a liar?'
Then all of a sudden the Head comes in
'You've been lying to Mrs Moody Pants here!
Ten detentions and one suspension
And pay attention to me!
No mobile phones and no Nintendos
And that's that!'

Niamh Krishman (9)
Our Lady Catholic Primary School, Hitchin

Farm Animals Are The Best

Farm animals are the best
They don't have hairy chests
Some moo and oink
And strangely point
Farm animals are the best.

Some farm animals are rather small
But some are rather tall
I can't quite tell
Which ones smell
Farm animals are the best.

Some farm animals are spotty
I even named one Dotty.
Black and white
They sometimes bite
Farm animals are the best.

Farm animals are the best
They are very good at chess
The farmer screams
While they all dream
Farm animals are the best.

Farm animals are the best
They always make a mess
But I still love them
I like to hug them
Farm animals are the best.

Bethan Simpson (9)
Our Lady Catholic Primary School, Hitchin

She Said

Miss, she said that I said that you said I said
But actually she said that I said, but I didn't!

Lauren Acosta-Clarke (9)
Our Lady Catholic Primary School, Hitchin

53

Dragons

Dragons are terrible beasts
But they do prepare a great feast
They come out in the night
To give you a fright
I saw one right on the scene.

I saw an army
They all had scales
So they were definitely males
I saw them right on the scene.

I knew a dragon called Dilly
Dilly was very silly
But then I saw something very odd
I knew it wasn't meant to be
I saw you on the scene.

Daniel O'Mahony (8)
Our Lady Catholic Primary School, Hitchin

My Best Friend

M y best friend sticks with me through thick and thin
Y et we never fall out

B est friends are for life
E very day we play together
S pecial friends are the best
T ogether we are the best

F eehan is her second name
R ose is her first
I n good time and bad we stay strong friends
E very day she is loyal to me
N ever apart, we stick like glue
D ay and night we stay together.

Grace Spillane (9)
Our Lady Catholic Primary School, Hitchin

On Ogolee Pogolee Land

On Ogolee Pogolee land
There was lots and lots of sand
Red, green and purple it may seem
On Ogolee Pogolee Land

On Ogolee Pogolee Land
There was a brilliant, brilliant band
With drums, guitars and George Sampson too
On Ogolee Pogolee land.

On Ogolee Pogolee Land
They wrote poems about their land
They go to bed at twelve precise
On Ogolee Pogolee Land.

Dale Bean (9)
Our Lady Catholic Primary School, Hitchin

Books

There are lots of different books
Each with characters with different looks
Some with characters that are mean
Some with characters that are lean
Some with characters that are manky
Some with characters that are cranky
Some with characters that are pretty
Some with characters that are witty
There are lots of different books
Everyone with different looks.

Esta Norton (9)
Our Lady Catholic Primary School, Hitchin

Space

Space is creepy, where you want to go with only the sun watching you.
You're sent there by NASA.
When you've reached there your heart beats faster than light
Mars forms with the sun to make Marun which chases you,
Venus burns you, Earth calms you,
Mercury destroys you and Jupiter
Budges and squeezes you,
And then you die with a big cry,
It feels like you'll fry.

Achintya Dhangar (9)
Our Lady Catholic Primary School, Hitchin

My Aunty

My aunty phoned yesterday
And this is what she shouted,
'You're going away today'
But I didn't know what she meant.

I asked my mum who said,
'You are going away today to Ireland of course,
Across the Irish Sea.'

I thought to myself, *by myself on a plane?*
What a long way for me, what might I see?

Niamh Adams (9)
Our Lady Catholic Primary School, Hitchin

Moody Monday

Miss is moody on Monday mornings
She is mean and doesn't give warnings
She will hit and kick until she's sick
If you hear a hummingbird she will jump and go ballistic!

Antonia Roberts (9)
Our Lady Catholic Primary School, Hitchin

Football

I like football the most
And not shooting on the goalpost.

When I see the football kit
I'm ready to be fit.

Our goalkeeper is the best
But his T-shirt's muddier than the rest.

Fans roaring, 'Goal, goal, goal!'
Soon after, 'More, more, more!'

Nadia Misztal (8)
Our Lady Catholic Primary School, Hitchin

Chocolate

Chocolate, chocolate, tasty and rich
White and brown, so many to pick
I like it soft, I like it hot
Sometimes I think I'm losing the plot.

Chocolate, chocolate, tasty and rich
Crispy and crunchy, so many to pick
I like it cold, I like it hard
Sometimes I think it looks like card.

Oliver Du Fou (9)
Our Lady Catholic Primary School, Hitchin

Horses

I like horses
They eat carrots, hay and grass.

I used to ride horses
It was such fun.

I want to ride them
All of the time.

Elise Clabburn (8)
Our Lady Catholic Primary School, Hitchin

Mystery Land

I came from a land far away
Where caravans and camels grow
Scorpions sit at your feet
And everyone wears a sheet.

So come on down, stop on by
Hop on a carpet and fly.
The wind from the east, the sun from the west
Will take you to this mysterious place.

Niamh Crawley (8)
Our Lady Catholic Primary School, Hitchin

Friends

F   is for friends who never let you down
R   is for relationships that friends have with you
I   is for I have a lot of friends, Tillie and Antonia are two
E   is for evening I go round to play
N   is for never which I will never ever lose my friends
D   is for Dale who is one of my best friends, sometimes we fight but
    our friendship never ends
S   is for super which my friends are, super duper!

Aoife McKeown (8)
Our Lady Catholic Primary School, Hitchin

Dark Mansion

Once upon a time there was a dark, dark mansion
In the dark, dark mansion was a rickety stairway.
Up the rickety stairway was a black room.
In the black room was a huge closet.
In the huge closet was a tatty box
In the tatty box was a piece of string.

Ross Matthews (9)
Our Lady Catholic Primary School, Hitchin

Little Bo Peep

Little Bo Peep
With knickers that bleep
Is looking for her stupid sheep
And they've gone with the sweep
And fallen asleep
Wagging their tails to the beat.

Mica Carrey (9)
Our Lady Catholic Primary School, Hitchin

My Dog

My dog is a nutty dog
He likes chasing logs
My dog is a silly dog
He likes chasing funny frogs.

Ciaron Taylor (9)
Our Lady Catholic Primary School, Hitchin

Polar Bears - Haikus

Polar bears are stars
Polar bears are good hunters
Polar bears are great.

Polar bears are white
Polar bears shine like diamonds
Polar bears are huge.

Polar bears are big
Polar bears are very cute
Polar bears are cute.

Polar bears are kind
Polar bears live in the cold
Polar bears are fun.

Phoebe Hing (9)
Our Lady of Lourdes RC Primary School, Stonebridge

Fire Rocks

A
Glam
On its own
Is not enough
For a little
Bit of
Glamour
And
Glimmer.
It will
Do its
Thing
That is
Why you
Are
Inspired
With it
Once again
Fireworks
Are
Cool
Buy
Them
And
Fly
Them.

Abel Semere (9)
Our Lady of Lourdes RC Primary School, Stonebridge

School Joy - Haiku

The school's filled with joy
I have fun I do in class
I have to behave.

Samuel Danquah (9)
Our Lady of Lourdes RC Primary School, Stonebridge

Countries

A mazing America
B rilliant Brazil
C unning Congo
D ramatic Denmark
E xtraordinary England
F antastic France
G orgeous Grenada
H orrific Hungary
I nteresting Italy
J olly Japan
K ind Kuala Lumpur
L ovely Luxembourg
M agical Morocco
N ew, New Zealand
O ptimistic Orlando
P olite Portugal
Q uiet Quebec
R elaxing Romania
S uper Spain
T remendous Thailand
U nbelievable Ukraine
V ibrating Vietnam.

Daniel Madeira Silva (9)
Our Lady of Lourdes RC Primary School, Stonebridge

Sweets

Sweets, sweets, you are so good.
Sweets, sweets, you are a treat.
Sweets, sweets, you make me smile.
Sweets, sweets, I can have you for a feast.
Sweets, sweets, I will be happy if I see ten of you.
Sweets, sweets, I can chew you forever.
Sweets, sweets, I can smell you from a mile away.
Sweets, sweets, can I be your friend?

Yosyef Alem (10)
Our Lady of Lourdes RC Primary School, Stonebridge

A Day In My Life

Walk to school today
In the wonderful sunshine
We are happy too.

I get up and wash
I get dressed, I eat a little
I leave, I say bye.

We wash together
We play like we are best friends
I like my best friends.

Today I want money
Money is my favourite thing
So I have it all.
I have a black dog
He likes to fight cats
He likes to catch cats

I see a robot
He is silver and very strong
I named him Jackson.

Dylan Danga Dje Oleko (8)
Our Lady of Lourdes RC Primary School, Stonebridge

My Dad's Old Car

Hum, hiss, caboom!
This car has got to go.
It's really quite old
It huffs, it puffs, it puffs, it huffs
Crackle, cough, whizz, wheee
I think it's going to freeze
One more turn and the car is going to fall into bitesize pieces.

D'Andre Clarke (8)
Our Lady of Lourdes RC Primary School, Stonebridge

Peppers

Red-hot smiling chillies going everywhere
You will still love them
Hot chilli in the summer breeze
Makes you smile
Makes you throw up!

Sarah Obi (9)
Our Lady of Lourdes RC Primary School, Stonebridge

Hanoi

Millions of motorbikes flowing down the street
Lots of friendly people on their way to work
Hotels, cafés, people sitting on tiny chairs drinking beer and soup
Headless fish, small cooked birds, shrimps swimming in bowls
There are narrow alleys between the stalls
Brilliantly coloured flowers, tulips, roses,
Weird fruit with weird names, dragon fruit?
Fireworks lighting up the black sky.

The stink of fish, I hate that smell!
All the herbs in a row, it smells so nice
Raw, red meat
Suffocating exhaust fumes
The noodle soup cooking in the street café
The sweet smell of tulips being sold by the bunch
Incense sticks smoking in a jar.

Engine revving
Horn blowing
Market traders shouting
Shops blaring loud foreign music
Sizzling food on the cooker
Fireworks exploding above the crowds.

The sights, the smells and the sounds of Hanoi are what I remember.

Rosie Clewett (10)
Ravenscroft Primary School, Plaistow

Nature

Nature is all around me
You don't need to get in with a key.
The smell of lovely flowers
Who sit under the sun for hours.
There are so many trees
Which get attracted by buzzy bees.

Children come from far away
They come for nature in the month of May.
They climb on trees
But they get stung by the buzzing bees.
Some children play games
While other children make daisy chains.

Some animals are clean
Although other animals sparkle like a beam.
Some animals have fun
While other animals lie down under the sun.
Some animals relax in the pool
While other animals feel cool.

Now I know nature is the best
All I can do now is have a rest.
Now you know how nature is
Go to nature in a fly of a whizz!

Saida Hussain (9)
Ravenscroft Primary School, Plaistow

Roses Are Red, Violets Are Blue

Roses are red, violets are blue
You are my mother and I love you.

Roses are red, violets are blue
You are my family and I trust you.

Rose are red, violets are blue
You give me care and lots of love too.

Asli Yusuf (9)
Ravenscroft Primary School, Plaistow

Princesses

Princesses are cute
They love to play a flute.
They shine so bight
And wear dresses that are white.

Princesses are smart
And they have a big heart.
She has someone special
And his name is Crecial.

Princesses are good
They don't eat too much food.
Princesses are nice
And they hate mice.

Princesses are sometimes funny
And they like to collect some money.
Princesses are sweet
And they like to have a treat.

Princesses are fun
And they like to make a bun.
Princesses are funny
And they like to have a bunny.

Lidia Dardai (9)
Ravenscroft Primary School, Plaistow

My Sister

My sister is good and never misunderstood.
My sister is lovely, she never picks her nose.
My sister eats food and is never in a mood.
My sister is cool and sunbathes.
My sister is sweet and very petite.
My sister, sister, sister, sister, sister.

Damilola Olanipekun-Allinson (8)
Ravenscroft Primary School, Plaistow

Me And My Friend

Me and my friend
Are the best friends of all
Nothing can break us
Not even a wall.

We go to the park
Have loads of fun
Go in the pool
And doze in the sun.

Cos me and my friend
Are best friends of all
Nothing can break us
Not even shopping at the mall.

We don't like football
But we love gymnastics
There are so many people
That are so elastic!

Cos me and my friend
Are best friends of all
Nothing can break us
Nothing at all.

Jola Bytyci (9)
Ravenscroft Primary School, Plaistow

Friends

My name is Zainab, I'm ten years old.
I am a very nice girl.
I entered this competition because writing is my whole world.
I have many friends and they appreciate me.
They have been my friends since the start,
Wherever they go they will always be in my heart.

Zainab Shittu (10)
Ravenscroft Primary School, Plaistow

A Perfect Day

A perfect day
Has to have lots of glee
A picnic in the park
Some honey from the bee.

A perfect day
Has a big part of fun
Across the beach
When Mum gives out the buns.

A perfect day
Is so sweet and so calm
When you hear brilliant stories
And the prince with his charm.

A perfect day
Is a time to go to sleep
Say goodnight to family
And end the wonderful day you can keep.

Neide Barbara Da Costa Feio (9)
Ravenscroft Primary School, Plaistow

Flowers

I think flowers are cute.
I think flowers are colourful.
I think flowers are beautiful.
I think flowers are soft.
Flowers are in different names.
I think flowers are like people in different sizes.
I think flowers are neat because they give us oxygen.
I think flowers are cool because they shine in the sun.
I think flowers are asleep when the moon has come.
I think flowers are like sisters to the bees.
I think flowers are pretty when they start to grow.
I think flowers are fantastic when they rise.
I think flowers are special because they make me think of you!

Sameenah Ahmed (8)
Ravenscroft Primary School, Plaistow

My Pet Dog

My dog is cool
He runs around the track
People bet on him
What do you think of that?
People cheer when he wins
But when he loses he has a boo.
No dog can beat him
Not on this whole Earth.
He races his whole life
And has trained so hard
Then he's put in a cage ready
For the next day.
He never used to be loved or cuddled too
But run around the track
Was what he had to do.
His life was hard and he had no fun
And I have him now, that's the best thing I've done.

Jade Mercer (11)
Ravenscroft Primary School, Plaistow

The Story Of Connie Gray

The first day I was born I was put into my mother's arms
The first thing I saw was this big necklace with shining beautiful charms.
I found out the way to get attention was to cry to get my own way
Mum would come running in and would open the curtains then I'd know it was a new day.
As the days went past my life began to go so fast
Then it came, my first birthday, I was growing up at last.

Here I am, my first day at school, I'm starting to think I'm growing tall
Let this be a day I'll always remember, now I've learnt my birthday's in December
I remember all those years, kisses and cuddles and tears.

Connie Gray (10)
Ravenscroft Primary School, Plaistow

Rice And Curry

Rice and curry
In a hurry
Grab your plate
Don't come too late
Otherwise
They'll be gone.

Rice and curry
In a hurry
Rice and curry
In a hurry
Taste too good
Come try it you should
I promise you
You will want more.

Rice and curry
In a hurry.

Safia Nadour (11)
Ravenscroft Primary School, Plaistow

Best Friends

B est friends forever
E at together
S chool together
T alk together

F un and games together
R iding bikes together
I ce creams together
E njoy sleepovers together
N o bad times together
D ance together
S tay best friends forever!

Amy Bartell (7)
Ravenscroft Primary School, Plaistow

My Pets

My cats like rats
But they don't like bats.

My dogs like sitting on logs
But they don't like frogs.

My shark likes dogs' barks
But he doesn't like my friend Mark.

My parrots like carrots
But they don't like Nick Sharratt.

My smallest pet is a mouse
It likes to hide in the house
But it doesn't like a green woodlouse.

These are all the pets I have
They all like different things like rats or frogs or maybe carrots
Which one do you like?

Melinda Hogman (8)
Ravenscroft Primary School, Plaistow

My Grandad

My grandad was a funny lad
He always made me laugh.
He was really kind all the time
He never ever used to shout at me.
He always used to call me Pinky Baby
Because I loved pink when I was a baby.
Unfortunately he passed away when I was three
I couldn't even see him properly.
It was sad because he never got to see my other cousins
It's not the same anymore without him.
When my grandma comes to my house I only see her, not my grandad
But that's how life is, everyone has to die at some point.
Grandad, I miss you.

Noushin Zaman Murshida (10)
Ravenscroft Primary School, Plaistow

70

My Wonderful Mother

It was my wonderful mother
Who sat and watched my infant head
When sleeping on my cradle bed
Affectionate with tears to shed,
My mother.

It was also my wonderful mother
When pains and sickness made me cry
Who gazed into my heavy eyes
With tears of fear that I should die,
My mother.

Oh my wonderful mother
How can I forget to be
Affectionate and kind to thee?
Who was so very kind to me,
My mother.

Ololade Busari (10)
Ravenscroft Primary School, Plaistow

Me And My Buddie

M e and Crystal
E ating chocolate

A nd having sleepovers
N ight and day
D eciding what we shall do

M e and Crystal
Y elling, 'Hi'

B oogying all around
U nder the scary ground
D igging into my ears
D ig, dig, dig
I nvestigating
E specially for me.

Aisha Mubaraq Balhweesal (8)
Ravenscroft Primary School, Plaistow

Funny Jokes

Funny jokes are sunny
They even make me eat some honey.
They make me eat cheese before bedtime
Or even snails with green slime.

Only funny jokes cannot be funny
When I drink my tea with lemon and honey.
When it's boiling and I drop it on the floor
Or when I say I'm skilful and close
My eyes and start to walk and crash my head to the door.

Well, you see, funny jokes cannot be funny
So don't follow me, don't eat cheese before bedtime
Don't eat honey
Don't eat snails with green slime!

Benjamin Lazar (10)
Ravenscroft Primary School, Plaistow

When I Grow Up To Ten

When I'm one I still have fun
When I'm two I'll still chew
When I'm three I'll still touch my knee
When I'm four I'll stay here a little bit more
When I'm five I'll still be alive
When I'm six I'll get some sticks
When I'm seven I'll go to Heaven
When I'm eight I'll still make
When I'm nine I'll still find
When I'm ten I'll see you again.

Zeibunnisha Omar (7)
Ravenscroft Primary School, Plaistow

Noisy Noises

There was a terrible hubbub - listen hark!
There was a terrible hubbub aboard Noah's ark.
The snakes were hissing, the bats were screeching,
The dogs were barking, the mice were squeaking,
The cats were purring, the bulls were tapping,
The cows were mooing, the starlings were flapping,
The wolves were howling, the crickets were creaking,
The elephants were stomping, the people were speaking.
After a while Noah gave a shout,
'If you don't stop that noise, you can all get out!'

Kiran Landa (11)
Ravenscroft Primary School, Plaistow

Milkshake, Milkshake

Milkshake, milkshake,
Bananas and milk.
Blend it all together
And shake very well.

Shake, shake,
Glurp, glurp,
It's in your belly now.
Now you want some more
You will have to milk the cow!

Gesibina Eneberi (11)
Ravenscroft Primary School, Plaistow

Night

Stars wander the skies
Like children who have lost their mother
Crying, ever lost
They are very clever
To hide from me in the day.

Saydul Islam (9)
Ravenscroft Primary School, Plaistow

Magic Is A Treat

Magic is a treat for fairies
And children? Get to go shopping
But that's not fair cos everybody should share magic
The fairies want to be part of our world
And we want them to be here
But the witch put the charm on the naughty nature fairy
But the children spotted it and got the fairy to fix it
Wow! That's a lot of light
All of a sudden the children and fairies were friends.

Isabel Prill (8)
Ravenscroft Primary School, Plaistow

Rhino

Bulky creature
Plant eater
Dung dropper
Two-horned
Of African savannah
What am I?
A: Rhino.

Jesse Hanson-Johnson (11)
Rockmount Primary School, Upper Norwood

Mice
(Inspired by 'Mice' by Rose Fyleman)

I think mice are rather nice
Their feet are small; they don't seem to have any ears at all.
Their tiddly tails have a mind of their own
Their big black eyes keep their secrets unknown.
They scurry across the floor so quickly you don't seem to notice
Their noses are cute and their whiskers thin as thread.
I don't see why people are so scared, because I think mice are rather
nice.

Deborah Hughes (11)
Rockmount Primary School, Upper Norwood

My Rabbit, Rayquaza

My rabbit, Rayquaza
He mostly watches TV.
My rabbit, Rayquaza
Is not always kind to me.
My rabbit, Rayquaza
Is not so cool you see.
He thinks he's tough,
When he's actually rough
And before he acted like a softy.
My rabbit, Rayquaza
Loves playing hide-and-seek.
He would hide
And could stay hidden for a week!
My rabbit, Rayquaza.
Is such a lazy bunny
He either eats and then sleeps
And dreams for the rest of the day.
In fact, my rabbit, Rayquaza
Isn't a rabbit at all!
He is just a dragon with bad habits
And that may sound cool.

Samuell Dago (11)
Rockmount Primary School, Upper Norwood

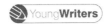

The Seasons

Winter
Winter comes, time to go to the park,
Gotta go early before it gets dark.
The pond is icy the ducks have left,
The leaves are gone there's been a theft!
It's Christmas soon, I just can't wait,
We watch TV and stay up late.
We crunch cream chocolates and munch mince pies
Then get ready for tomorrow to bring a surprise.
The next day it's snowing, the presents are here,
We sit down at the table and give a big cheer.

Spring
The curtains are open; the sun has been shown,
The sky is bright blue and the lawn has been mown.
The flowers are open; there are leaves on the trees,
There are sounds of birds singing and buzzing of bees.
The blossoms are blooming; the sun's shining bright,
The grass is bright green, it's a beautiful sight!
Soon Easter will come with chocolate galore
With Mars eggs, Maltesers, white chocolate and more.
A great time for picnics and dips in the pool,
I don't need to say that spring's hot yet sill cool.

Summer
School's stopped; let's go play outside in the sun
You can hear children laughing whilst they have fun.
Gotta go shopping so we can party till late
Sending out invites with the time and the date.
We're going away somewhere to tan
Spain or Italy, I'm an ice cream fan.
Let's swim in the sea, collect lots of shells,
See all the sights and build castles as well.
Deck out in cool gear, like T-shirts and shorts
Get a good pair of shades and get involved in some sports.

Autumn
Jump in the leaves all over the floor
With them all floating around you in awe.

Get a good suit so you can go trick or treat
It's Hallowe'en soon, lots of chocolate and sweets.
School's starting again and you get a new class
Your first piece of work which won't be your last!
The days get shorter, they also get cold
The nights get longer; nature still has its hold.
It's Bonfire Night watch the sparks in the sky
Standing there watching the sparks reflect in your eyes.

Eloise Jeary (11)
Rockmount Primary School, Upper Norwood

A Strange Night

In a scary dark night
Cars cruise one another
Fast and noisy as if they were
Lions, tigers, elephants, snakes
In front a crocodile-mouth tunnel
Swallowing everything
Cat eyes dazzle on the large road
When jaguar cars pass by
Street lights flicker and fall
Like a flock of birds
Herds of people shy away
From car beasts.

Gustavo Camarotte (11)
Rockmount Primary School, Upper Norwood

Greeny, My Old Friend

Small-footed
As thin as pencil lead
Really cute
Loves the flute
Climbs on trees
He's allergic to bees
Likes a Sunday lay in
Green scales
His favourite toy is the whale
He's a great friend
Until the end.

Paris Brock (11)
Rockmount Primary School, Upper Norwood

The Saw Ride

Start as a zigzag
Feeling scared to come off
You are still
Your heart is beating while
You go up, up, up in silence
You're on the tip of the ride
Terrified of the height
Suddenly you crash down
The force is strong and hard
Sharply spinning while you curl
Then it's over.

Du'chey Doyley Laing (11)
Rockmount Primary School, Upper Norwood

Guess Who I Am

Hay fever bringer
Wedding giver
Park destroyer
Holiday sender
Beach packer
Ice cream melter
Human sweat bags
With all the fashion mags
Sunburn receiver
Rather than iceberg cooler.

Joanna Kazibwe (11)
Rockmount Primary School, Upper Norwood

Football

Football team players
The cheering crowd
A goalkeeper's tricks
A score, noises loud.

The ball is like a bullet
A player's foul tackle
A shrill referee's whistle
And the crowd heckle!

Damion Hawthorne (11)
Rockmount Primary School, Upper Norwood

Clothing

Sometimes yellow
Sometimes green
Rain repellent
Always keen
To keep you warm
In a storm
What am I?
A: A raincoat.

Julien Mahe Crenn (10)
Rockmount Primary School, Upper Norwood

The Maid That Cleans My House

Bed maker
Vacuum diva
Window cleaner
Shoe polisher
Garden planter
Breakfast maker
What am I?
A: A Maid.

Saleha Akhtar (10)
Rockmount Primary School, Upper Norwood

Boring

B ored of doing the same thing
O ngoing subjects each day
R olling, boring and simple stuff
I nvolving some subjects
N othing new each day
G oing to school is boring!

Joseph Adusei (11)
St John's CE Primary School, Penge

The Big City's Future

The big city is like a cage
Holding everything inside it with skyscraper walls
The cars move slowly leaving a poisonous trail
Helplessly gliding along the streams of gravel.

People rushing about like it is the end of the world
Buying things they do not need in shops
Sniffing perfumes, leaving them hypnotised to buy every scent
Spending so much money, we are wasting it, letting it wash away.

Animals destroy everything, innocently chewing
Streams dry up leaving fish to rot
Children run and scream
Then there is silence.

The big city is abandoned
Cars and rubbish are dotted everywhere
Houses are empty in the quiet streets
A silent breeze floats through the cage.

Clare Symons (11)
St John's CE Primary School, Penge

Abandoned

'Please don't leave me,
Will you stay?
Mummy left me,
She went away.

I thought that she
Would be back soon,
But I have sat here
From night to noon.

And my mummy
Never came.
Will I ever
See her again?'

Jadzia Samuel (11)
St John's CE Primary School, Penge

I Love My Mum

My mum loves me and I love her
Up and ready just for me
Me and my mum have such great times
Always together to make us happy, no one's better than my mum
She is the best mum in the world!

Olivia Tizie (9)
St John's CE Primary School, Penge

Envy

Envy is black and rocky
Envy tastes of cold blood and raw carrots
Envy smells of betrayal and a dead mouse
                    who is rotting and armpit sweat
Envy looks like flames from Hell and mouldy cheese
Envy sounds like the scraping of nails on metal screws
                        and cries for help from Hell
Envy sounds like a squeak which is constantly tunnelling into
                            your ears
Envy feels like your heart and lungs being torn out with anger
Envy feels like blood gushing out your brain
Whilst you're being hammered.

Flora-Rose Nyembwe (11)
St Joseph's RC Primary School, Willesden

Joy

Joy is the colour of light blue
The taste of joy is like a crunchy sweet apple
Joy smells like new-baked muffins
Joy looks like best friends laughing and joking
It is like birds humming in the trees
Joy feels like fluffy bunnies hugging you
I love joy.

Jamie-Lee Walsh (9)
St Joseph's RC Primary School, Willesden

Happiness And Sadness

Happiness is fluffy, pink and red
It tastes like juicy strawberries
Happiness smells like fresh flowers
And crunchy red apples
Happiness feels like a hug from my mum.

Sadness is grey and dark
It tastes like rotten bananas
And smells like burnt toast
Sadness looks like dead rats
And sounds like the sewers
Sadness feels really gloomy.

Cherise Roche-Ross (10)
St Joseph's RC Primary School, Willesden

Fear

Fear is pitch-black
It tastes like sour blood burning in your mouth
As if you are being poisoned
It smells like a rotting bird being eaten away by flesh-eating maggots
It looks like staring at the Devil in the eye, as if you are in Hell
It sounds like the screams of people killed in the deadly, Civil War
It feels like being tortured in Alcatraz
With the innocent tortured spirits circling around you.
Fear panics me!

Andrew Da Silva (11)
St Joseph's RC Primary School, Willesden

Hate

Hate is grey
Hate is the colour of the sky when it rains
Hate is the Devil
Hate is like mouldy, smelly cheese
Hate tastes like out of date sweets
Hate smells like thunder burning a house to the ground
Hate sounds like thunder roaring in the sky
Hate feels like a hard rock being thrown
Hate makes me mad.

Rohan Hoo-Kim (10)
St Joseph's RC Primary School, Willesden

Fear

Fear is dark
Fear is black
Fear is the work of evil
Fear is terrible
Fear is destruction to all
Fear smells of dead animals
Fear tastes like mouldy fear
If you see it, hide your soul
Before it kills you.

Kevin Lopes De Almeida (11)
St Joseph's RC Primary School, Willesden

Beauty

Beauty is the colour of shimmering plums
It tastes like raspberry ice cream from the sweet shop
Beauty smells like sweet, glittering perfumes
It looks like a sugar-coated sweet cake
Beauty sounds like smooth, relaxing music
Beauty is like a spa shop!

Natalia Cichon (10)
St Joseph's RC Primary School, Willesden

Jealousy Is Juicy

Jealousy is blood-red
It tastes like a sour, bitter lime
And smells like a plague rat from the sewers
Jealousy looks like a spiteful devil
And sounds like a bagpipe squeaking in my ear
Jealousy makes my blood boil
And it feels like I'm going to explode
Jealousy is juicy.

Kerri O'Toole (11)
St Joseph's RC Primary School, Willesden

Hunger

Hunger is pitch-black
It tastes like bitter acid
It smells like burning metal
And looks like fiery sparks of black coal
It sounds like defeat
And feels like despair
Hunger is delusional
And hunger frightens me.

Acayo Okello (11)
St Joseph's RC Primary School, Willesden

Anger

Anger is dark red
It tastes like burning stones
And smells like smoke from Hell
Anger looks like an enraged volcano
It sounds like thunder crashing
Anger feels like fire from Hades
I hate anger
It makes me full of rage!

Maleusz Jarecki (10)
St Joseph's RC Primary School, Willesden

YoungWriters

Loyalty

Loyalty is a loving, shimmering *gold*
It tastes like sweet, sugary biscuits
And smells like a colourful bouquet of flowers
Loyalty looks like a soft, fluffy pillow
It sounds like one thousand people
Playing sweet, sparkling songs on the violin
Loyalty feels like you're on top of the world
Loyalty is fantastic!

Amarni Lee (10)
St Joseph's RC Primary School, Willesden

Laughter

Baby-blue is laughter
It tastes like creamy white chocolate
And smells like yummy baked cookies
I see people laughing and joking together
It feels like sleeping on a queen's bed
And wearing a golden crown
It sounds like birds humming together
Laughter is the best!

Zhane Gilbert Smith (10)
St Joseph's RC Primary School, Willesden

Fear

Fear is deathly black
It tastes like cold, red blood
And smells like damp, cold air
Fear is like a pack of bloodthirsty wolves
It sounds like a heartbeat drumming in your ear
Fear is like a cold breath of air touching your neck
I hate fear!

Matthew Cleary (11)
St Joseph's RC Primary School, Willesden

86

Loneliness

Loneliness is a pale, boring blue
It tastes like a rotten pea, slowly decaying
And smells like pollution from the back of a truck's exhaust just
revving its engine
Loneliness looks like a teardrop of sadness dropping on the ground
And sounds as if a pencil is drawing a never-ending line alone
Loneliness feels like nothing to feel . . . nothing with no one!

Liam Wall (9)
St Joseph's RC Primary School, Willesden

Envy

Envy is bogey-green
Envy tastes like a poisonous apple
And smells like a stinky, sweaty sock
It looks like a venomous snake slithering through the dark
Envy sounds like an evil witch's laughter
Envy feels like a dark cloud gloating above your head
Envy is *cruel!*

Andrea Arhagba (10)
St Joseph's RC Primary School, Willesden

Love

Love is shiny, ruby-red
It tastes like a night on the sea
And smells like red roses
Love looks like two love birds sitting on a pink cloud
It sounds like a heart pumping
Love feels like two fluffy bunnies hugging
I love love!

Kayleigh McCarthy (10)
St Joseph's RC Primary School, Willesden

Joy

Joy is the colour of bright sunshine
It tastes like scrumptious sweets
And it smells like my mum's best perfume
Joy looks like two people in love
Joy sounds like people laughing on a summer's day
Joy makes me think of beautiful roses
I love joy!

Ricardo Deniro German (10)
St Joseph's RC Primary School, Willesden

Sadness

Sadness is deep coral-blue
It tastes like bitter lemons
Sadness smells like a river of tears
And looks like children in despair . . .
It sounds like a baby sobbing
Sadness is a cold wind whistling down your spine
Sadness is horrible.

Ellie Louise Woodford (10)
St Joseph's RC Primary School, Willesden

Laughter

Laughter is the colour of an orange pumpkin
It tastes like fresh, sweet toffees
Laughter smells like a burger getting cooked at a barbecue
It looks like fairies bouncing on marshmallows
Laughter sounds like the sizzling of scrambled eggs on toast
Laughter feels like licking a cold, minty ice cream
I love laughter!

Samuel Macauley (10)
St Joseph's RC Primary School, Willesden

Hunger!

Hunger is dark grey
It tastes like nothingness
Hunger smells like a dark, damp tunnel
It looks like an endless hole dug in the ground
Hunger sounds like fifty banshees wailing at once
It feels like the end of the world
Hunger is horrible!

Alice Mullahy (11)
St Joseph's RC Primary School, Willesden

Loneliness

Loneliness is the colour grey
Very sad and dim
It tastes like bitter fish
It smells like gone off broccoli
It looks like a thundercloud
It sounds like an explosive bomb
The feeling is very cold . . .

Matthew Brandon Halpin (10)
St Joseph's RC Primary School, Willesden

Loneliness

Loneliness is deep night-blue
It tastes of sour blueberries
And smells like wet feet on a miserable day
Loneliness looks like a baby crying
It sounds like children locked in a room, screaming
Loneliness feels like you're hated
I don't like loneliness!

Afiya Knights (10)
St Joseph's RC Primary School, Willesden

Love!

Love is ruby-red
It tastes like fresh, ripe strawberries
Love smells like expensive perfume in the air
With kindness and happiness
It looks like stars, shining in the night
And sounds like sweet music
Love feels like a touch of happiness.

Isabelle Salomao (10)
St Joseph's RC Primary School, Willesden

Joy

Joy is bright yellow
It tastes like the biscuits from the Harlesden bakery
Joy smells like flowers in a massive field
It looks like dangling angels high up in the sky
Joy sounds like the church bells ringing
It feels like I'm jumping on fluffy marshmallows
I'm full of joy!

Krystian Tlak (10)
St Joseph's RC Primary School, Willesden

Hate

Hate is dark red
It tastes like mouldy cheese
It smells like a revolting dead rat
It looks like people fighting in the street
It sounds like shouting and screaming
It feels horrible and so, so sad
Hate is the worst thing in my life.

Chloe MacLeod (10)
St Joseph's RC Primary School, Willesden

Love

Love:
Love is the colour of a red rose
Red is the colour of my mum's lipstick
It tastes like Mum's loving kiss
It smells like a mother's floating fragrance
It sounds like Miley Cyrus' song 'Breakout'
It feels like Valentine's Day.

Judith Elhendi (10)
St Joseph's RC Primary School, Willesden

Anger

Is not a very nice black
It tastes like a cactus on your tongue
And smells worse than a pig sty
It looks like a face is ruby-red
It is torture to the ears
It feels like you're going to blow,
5, 4, 3, 2, 1, let's go!

Emmanuel Amoah Acheampong (9)
St Joseph's RC Primary School, Willesden

Deception

Being deceived is like being pierced in the heart
By those you thought were close to you
Deception is the scum beneath your shoes
And the germs when you sneeze
But being deceived is the most mortifying thing
Red is the colour of envy, which triggers deception
I renounce deception!

Dijon Grey (11)
St Joseph's RC Primary School, Willesden

Loneliness

Loneliness is white
It tastes like blood
It smells smoky and damp
Loneliness looks like death
It sounds oh so quiet . . .
It feels sad and has a deep impact
On the way you're feeling.

Kevin Ceazer Valencia (10)
St Joseph's RC Primary School, Willesden

Beauty

Beauty is the colour of a rainbow in the blue sky
It tastes as sweet as sugar on strawberries
Beauty smells like roses in the morning light
It looks like stars twinkling in the night sky
Beauty sounds like birds twittering in a tree up high
Beauty feels nice and warm.

Catia Esteves (10)
St Joseph's RC Primary School, Willesden

Happiness

Happiness is here in every colour
Tasting so joyful
It smells like roses
Filling every bit of me
It sounds happy and loving
Happiness has arrived.

Aine Mackin (10)
St Joseph's RC Primary School, Willesden

Love Is Great!

Love is like a rainbow, a sign of happiness
It's like butterflies in your belly dying to come out any second
It smells of fresh air
And tastes like diamonds and gold in your mouth
It feels like a smooth, cold, cotton pillow you can rest on
It's like Heaven, but really, really colourful.

Joshua Joseph Devanney (11)
St Joseph's RC Primary School, Willesden

Happiness

Happiness is bright yellow like the beautiful sun
It tastes like a wonderful yellow lemon pudding
Happiness smells like a rose after the fresh rain
And looks like the birds singing with the bright sunrise
It sounds like a hummingbird in the sky
Happiness feels like a beach at sunrise.

Pedro Rodrigues (10)
St Joseph's RC Primary School, Willesden

A Sense Of Happiness

Happiness is blue
The taste of fresh apples on a fully grown tree
It smells like roses on a sunny summer day
And an exotic flower bed
It sounds like fun and laughter everywhere
Happiness makes me feel like I am on a beach holiday.

Raphael Makuba Rominique (10)
St Joseph's RC Primary School, Willesden

93

Love

Love is the colour red
The taste of nice juicy cherries
Love is the smell ot red roses
You can't stop feeling the love
It's so romantic.
Best life ever!

Hulda Mdorbasi (10)
St Joseph's RC Primary School, Willesden

Fear!

Fear is pitch-black
It tastes like the antidote to poison
And smells like old rotten garbage
Fear looks like the living dead
The sound of faint, ghostly voices pleading for help
Fear is paranormal . . .

Fábio José Dantas Fernandes (11)
St Joseph's RC Primary School, Willesden

Sweetest Love

Love smells like a branch of a red rose
Love tastes like when you eat chocolate hearts
Love looks like when your heart is beating harder
It feels like a beautiful girl walking past
The emotion is you just want to kiss a girl.

Olaf Trusiak (10)
St Joseph's RC Primary School, Willesden

Loneliness

Loneliness is dark black with an evil red spirit
It smells like a dark rainy day
And acts like shocking electricity
It makes me sad
Leave me alone!

Henrique Lourenco (11)
St Joseph's RC Primary School, Willesden

Epitaph

Why, oh why is life so short?
If I could I would have bought
About one more hour of my days
To fix all the mistakes I made
And tell the ones I really love
When I'm dead and up above
When my light has flickered out
I love you all, without a doubt.

Maisie Green-Buck (11)
The Wroxham School, Potters Bar

There Is A Mean Girl In My Class

There is a mean girl in my class
She is very mean
I can tell you that
She says things
Behind people's backs
She pretends to like me
But she doesn't
She only likes one person
In my class
And no one likes her
I wonder why?

Gabrielle Lay (10)
Watton at Stone Primary & Nursery School, Watton at Stone

World War II

World War II
Bombs
Cruel, quick
Frightening, deafening, destroying
Homes through to the ground
Explosion

Soldiers
Strong, fierce
Risking, killing, dying
Giving up their lives for their country
Men

Spitfire
Fast, dodgy
Flying, shooting, succeeding
Aeroplane

Children
Scared, small
Crying, screaming, confused
Hoping they would see their family again
The next generation.

Toby Thompson (11)
Watton at Stone Primary & Nursery School, Watton at Stone

PlayStation

PlayStations are the best
Lots of games to play
Amazing things can happen
You can do funny things
Some people are good or bad
Tick-tock goes the clock
It's time to stop
Oh no
Not now, just one more level!

George Neate (8)
Watton at Stone Primary & Nursery School, Watton at Stone

No One Wants Me

All alone
On my own
I don't want him
I hear whistling
Then I'm missing
I don't want him
Everyone's gone
The journey's been long
I don't want him
Evacuation
Isolation
I don't want him
I'm one of the last to be picked
No one will be tricked
I don't want him
My family I miss
I won't get another kiss
I don't want him
Held together
By a letter.

Evalyn Goldby Solomon (11)
Watton at Stone Primary & Nursery School, Watton at Stone

Peace

Peace is the wish of my life that I love
Peace is the wish of hope
Peace is on a boat
Peace is carried in a cart
Peace is in everybody's heart
And everyone's not letting go
Peace is a baby sleeping
Like a boat floating in the ocean
Peace is the gift of keeping
Like sticky weed, not letting go.

Billi Jo Beach (10)
Watton at Stone Primary & Nursery School, Watton at Stone

Nature

Nature, nature
Nobody hates ya
The slimy worm
Which makes people squirm
The leaping frog
Down by the bog.

Nature, nature
Nobody hates ya
The gliding bird
And patterns that are observed
A spider's web I spy
The spider has caught a fly.

Nature, nature
Nobody hates ya
The weeping willow
As soft as a pillow
The scaly fish running down the stream
That is the sort of thing that is in your dream.

Lydia Hardcastle (10)
Watton at Stone Primary & Nursery School, Watton at Stone

Evacuation

Today I left my mother crying
On the train I am crying
Tomorrow my sisters will be crying
Lost in the hall
Someone steps in
She takes us
Seeing her car
Thinking we are lucky
At the house we are lucky
Will we see our mum again?
If we're lucky.

Joe Wing (11)
Watton at Stone Primary & Nursery School, Watton at Stone

Under The Stair

Under the stair
Lies a terrible scare
Oh, I wish it wasn't there
Under the stair.

Under the stair
It's a bit like a bear
What a terrible scare
Under the stair.

Under the stair
Is a mop of green hair
I hope nothing's there
Under the stair.

Under the stair
Its jaw is bare
Go away horrible scare
Under the stair.

Megan Parlow (10)
Watton at Stone Primary & Nursery School, Watton at Stone

Snowing Tears

Every drop of snow
Is a rain-filled tear
Sitting on the earth
Cold and bare.

It has no jacket
To keep it warm
It has no protection
From the storm.

Melting away
Into the ground
Fast asleep
Without a sound.

Francesca Lane (11)
Watton at Stone Primary & Nursery School, Watton at Stone

99

School

Lesson one has just begun
Six, seven, eight, nine, ten.

Play now, yeah, wow
Whizz, yell, slip, ow!

Lesson two, oh boo-hoo
A, B, C, D, E . . .

Lunch now, woo, wow
Munch, yum, slurp, burp.

Lesson three, yay - PE
Run, jump, sprint, leap.

Lesson four, shut the door
Violin, piano, drum, guitar.

Time to go
To start the school cycle tomorrow.

Charlie Smith (10)
Watton at Stone Primary & Nursery School, Watton at Stone

Sweets

Sweets are lovely
Sweets are nice
Sweets are tasty
Sweets are tangy.

Sweets are sugary
Sweets are crunchy
Sweets are delicious
Sweets are chewy.

Sweets are sharp
Sweets are fruity
Sweets are sour
Sweets are fizzy.

Joanna Wood (10)
Watton at Stone Primary & Nursery School, Watton at Stone

Peace And War

Peace is a rope that binds us in friendship
A welcome fire on a stormy night
Peace is a smile-bringer, the builder and maker
Peace is the shield that protects us from fights.
It is the founder, the maker, the builder, creator.
Peace is the soft voice that lulls the monster
Into a deep and dark sleep, welcomed by all.

War is the life-taker, grief-maker
It destroys things that others have made.
War is a fire that burns the rope that was helping us all
A monster rampaging, creating destruction,
Destroying the friendships which had slowly been made.
War is a burden, upon weak shoulders
One that can easily drop and fall
Creating an explosion, hated by all.

Bryn Goodman (11)
Watton at Stone Primary & Nursery School, Watton at Stone

Horrible Histories

Horrible histories
Terrible Tudors
Gorgeous Georgians
Slimy Stuarts
Vile Victorians
Vicious Vikings
Creepy crimes

Rotten Romans
Ferocious fights
Daring knights
Horrors that defy
Your souls.

Ben Ellis (7)
Watton at Stone Primary & Nursery School, Watton at Stone

Sleepovers

A girly giggle, a boyish bounce
Sleepovers are the best
Sleeping bags, a blow-up bed
Sleepovers are the best!

Sweets, chocolate, fizzy drinks
Sleepovers are the best
Crisps, biscuits, fairy cakes
Sleepovers are the best.

Telling jokes, embarrassing moments
Sleepovers are the best
Reading books, magazines
Sleepovers are the best.

Silence falls like a dark shadow
Sleep at last!

Catherine New (9)
Watton at Stone Primary & Nursery School, Watton at Stone

War

War is a rampaging wreckage
It cannot be contained in a cage
War can last for years and years
But always often ends in tears
War creates a lot of dying
Also a lot of crying.

Every man has a gun
But it's not all that much fun
If a soldier is weak
They wouldn't think they're meek
Each soldier has to do his part
It's a work of art.

Joshua Allen (11)
Watton at Stone Primary & Nursery School, Watton at Stone

World War II

W orld of remorse
O ut of ammo
R ussia conquered
L umping on the floor
D ead on the ground

W ar in Italy
A t Jamaica
R oman slaves

T o war attack
W ar of the world
O uter line attack.

Jordan Russell (8)
Watton at Stone Primary & Nursery School, Watton at Stone

Animals

There are so many animals in the world
How do you remember them all?

Some are slow, some are tall
Some are fast, some are small
Some are noisy, some are scary
Some are quiet, some are hairy
Some are slimy, some are shy
Some are scaly, some can fly.

As you can see there are so many animals
How you do remember them all?

Rosa Alcantara (10)
Watton at Stone Primary & Nursery School, Watton at Stone

Gurty

My guinea pig's name is Gurty
She is chestnut-brown and black
Her cage is very dirty
Enough poop to fill a sack
She lays all day and sleeps at night
She eats all her food, but she never bites
She plays in her tunnel all the time
We always clean her out, but she never seems to mind
Whatever the weather, whenever the day
Who really cares as long as she's the same.

Jasmine Jenkins (9)
Watton at Stone Primary & Nursery School, Watton at Stone

My Imaginary Friend

I had an imaginary friend
When I was four, five and six
She was a part of my heart
I would give her a carrot at teatime
I used to wake her up in the morning
And put her to sleep at night
But then I forgot about her
My heart is in two
But I have remembered her now
And the cycle will start again.

Josie Bell (9)
Watton at Stone Primary & Nursery School, Watton at Stone

FBI

I know a guy
In the FBI
He flies in the sky
In his BBI.

Billy Wilkinson (9)
Watton at Stone Primary & Nursery School, Watton at Stone

104

WWII Evacuation

E motions flying like a bird in the sky
V ision blinded without my mum
A nger, distraught, with pain
C ourage never lost
U nited countries fighting for freedom
A unts waving goodbye
T rains travelling to peaceful countryside
I nstructions given
O pposite sides fighting for power
N ever-ending stream of tears.

Sunny Lee (11)
Watton at Stone Primary & Nursery School, Watton at Stone

Peace

Peace is the break of dawn
Peace is how you get warned
You need peace to go to sleep
Peace is like a twinkling street
Peace is like the night-time sky
You can have peace without even one try
You get peace when you go on a cruise ship
You just need to wiggle your hips
Peace is like being in your own home
Peace is when you get off the phone.

Tia-Mae Wessels (11)
Watton at Stone Primary & Nursery School, Watton at Stone

Puppies

Puppies are small
Puppies are cute
Puppies are so much fun
To play with too!

Eathan Vallance (10)
Watton at Stone Primary & Nursery School, Watton at Stone

Goodbye Mum

I had my breakfast, cheese on toast
My mum was crying and scared
This may be the last time I see her standing there

As I put on my coat and shoes
And pick up my bag ready to go
She kisses me and tells me how much she'll miss me so

Now it's time to say our sad farewells
Goodbye, goodbye, goodbye
Our hearts are gone.

Ben Stockley (10)
Watton at Stone Primary & Nursery School, Watton at Stone

Dogs

Dogs are silly
Dogs are big
Dogs are small
Dogs chase cats and chew hats
Dogs, dogs, dogs.

Some dogs
Don't like to play
They run around like a wild thing
Then come back inside.

Roisin Wilkinson (7)
Watton at Stone Primary & Nursery School, Watton at Stone

Penguins

Plump penguins, oh so friendly
Jump into water, oh so gracefully
Glide through the water like some swallows
Fly through the water like the Red Arrows
Penguins, penguins, penguins.

Rose Shepherd (9)
Watton at Stone Primary & Nursery School, Watton at Stone

Friend

A friend is helpful, kind and thoughtful
They will put you before themselves
They will always be there for you
And they will never let you down.

A friend is helpful, kind and thoughtful
They will be fair to you
They will help you if you need it
And they will go through all your troubles with you
This is what I think a friend is.

Megan Kinch (10)
Watton at Stone Primary & Nursery School, Watton at Stone

Goodbye

I hated being in London
It was like being in a dungeon
I waited for the train
Did I really feel the pain?

I inhaled the smell of the countryside
Although it had nearly died
The bombs, the noise, I cannot abide
I shared a kiss with my mum
And now that's all that needs to be done.

Charlotte Davidge (11)
Watton at Stone Primary & Nursery School, Watton at Stone

Liverpool

Liverpool are the best
They've won about 1,000 times
I like them
They're the best team in the world
And no other team can beat them.

Brandon Ashley-Haylock (10)
Watton at Stone Primary & Nursery School, Watton at Stone

Hallowe'en

Hallowe'en, scary things,
Spiders, vampires, bats with wings

Hallowe'en, scary stuff
Witches' spells, *piff, paff, puff.*

Hallowe'en, scary tales
Creepy noises, screams and wails.

Hallowe'en, scary night
Trick or treat gives me a fright.

Adam Phillips (10)
Watton at Stone Primary & Nursery School, Watton at Stone

Chocolate

C hocolate is yummy
H ow much do you eat?
O ne chocolate bun
C ute and tasty
O nly mine
L ovely treat
A nnouncing chocolate
T asty treat
E at me, eat me!

Harry Gogol (9)
Watton at Stone Primary & Nursery School, Watton at Stone

Summer

Summer, a wonderful season
Summer, stones as grey as an elephant's skin
Summer, pebbles as smooth as a table
Summer, seaweed as smelly as cheese
Summer, sea as clear as glass
Summer, piers as long as roads.

Anna Whittle (9)
Watton at Stone Primary & Nursery School, Watton at Stone

That Day (Evacuation WWII)

I see my mum fading away in the smoke
And still I can't remember the last time we spoke
I smell the lost joy scrambling in the stream
And now I feel like a lost member of the team
I hear the cry of the smallest child
And so I don't feel quite so mild
I feel the pain in my mum's throat as she calls
And of course, now I have no joy left in me at all
On that day.

Elysia Helena Moncur-Byrne (11)
Watton at Stone Primary & Nursery School, Watton at Stone

Ice Snow

I ce rink, you are skating around
C old, chilly coolness
E legantly beautiful

S loppy, slushy, wet and cold
N ice, cold, hard or soft
O ne snowball, two snowballs, three snowballs
  Pow!
W ow, it's a winter wonderland.

James Cuerden (10)
Watton at Stone Primary & Nursery School, Watton at Stone

The Evacuation

Everyone was crying, but the tears started drying
Everyone holding gas masks and even carrying mini flasks
There was some time to say goodbye, but the time really did fly
Everybody got on the train, crying loudly with great pain
When we reached the countryside, everybody shouted and cried
As we got up and off the train, we all wondered if we'd go home again.

Ryan Kelly (11)
Watton at Stone Primary & Nursery School, Watton at Stone

No Time To Say Goodbye

No time to say goodbye
How the children did all cry
We used to go out to play
How those days passed away
As we stepped upon the train
That's when I began to feel the pain
As we went to different places
I saw the tears on children's faces.

Robyn Neal (11)
Watton at Stone Primary & Nursery School, Watton at Stone

Today Is The Day

Waking up, today is the day
I'll leave my parents, what will I say?
Upset and distraught, I'm crying with fear
While my mother's saying, 'Look after yourself dear.'
I'm holding hands for the last time
War is a terrible, nasty crime
From the platform, onto the train
Leaving my mother full of pain.

Bethany Cooke (11)
Watton at Stone Primary & Nursery School, Watton at Stone

City And Noise

City is the place to go
Is the place where people say hello
The city is full of stalls and shops
Yes, where everyone loves to go
Everyone loves the shops
Now the place is open
Do you like it now it's open?
Now there's load of noise.

Eleanor York (8)
Watton at Stone Primary & Nursery School, Watton at Stone

110

Football

F antastic football
O pen arms
O pen legs
T hrough the legs
B reaking the net
A bout to score
L oser
L oser, on the floor.

Bradleigh Goldby Solomon (8)
Watton at Stone Primary & Nursery School, Watton at Stone

Weird Football

Nets, fouls
Cards, scoring
Players offside
Shots saved
Goals are fouls
Corners, goals
Now that's what
Football is all about.

Thomas Adams (9)
Watton at Stone Primary & Nursery School, Watton at Stone

Football

F ootball went over the bar
O pen arms
O pen legs
T hrough your legs
B all over your head
A bout to hit you
L ots of people in the stadium
L ots of people on the pitch.

Benjamin Borlase (8)
Watton at Stone Primary & Nursery School, Watton at Stone

Dreaming

D elightful dreaming
R eally lovely snuggled up in bed
E ven chocolate trains are here
A eroplanes are the best because they're made of fudge
M arvellous
I love to dream
N othing will stop me
'G et out of bed,' shouts Mum.

Marlee Hart (9)
Watton at Stone Primary & Nursery School, Watton at Stone

Ferrari

Fast and furious
Noisy and nosy
Speed and sound
Whoosh
There it goes
The
Ferrari
Enzo.

James Wood (9)
Watton at Stone Primary & Nursery School, Watton at Stone

Football

F ootball is my favourite sport
O n the school field, where I play it every day
O n my trampoline with a sponge ball I play it all the time
T -shirts are all Arsenal
B rother trying to score against my excellent keeping
A rsenal scoring absolute screamers
L acking sometimes, but always coming back
L uck is not what we need, we have power.

Edward Spratt (10)
Watton at Stone Primary & Nursery School, Watton at Stone

Leopard

Leopards are cuddly, spotty and fierce
But leopards live in hot countries
Some are big and some are small
Some are cubs and some are leopards
Some are cute, some are scary
Some are clever, some are dumb
Some live in the wild, some live in the zoo
Some could be as small as my thumb.

Miriam Tabone (8)
Watton at Stone Primary & Nursery School, Watton at Stone

Teeny Tots

Teeny tots are teeny weenie people
That are made out of jelly
They don't wear clothes
Or underwear
They just grow hair
I wonder why they like being called teeny tots
They could have been born that way
Or they could have just lost the plot.

Rhiannon Evans (8)
Watton at Stone Primary & Nursery School, Watton at Stone

Football

Running, sprinting everywhere I go
I'm so happy playing football
It's so much fun when I score
I celebrate
Kicking, hoping
It will get there
So I guess you can say
I love *football!*

Harvey Deards (8)
Watton at Stone Primary & Nursery School, Watton at Stone

Batman Fat Man

Batman is a fat man
He is a lazy man with a wiggly wand
And flying is not his thing
Too tired to fly he falls down from the sky
He lands on a building, flat on his face
Too big to go through the door
Too big to eat any more
Too large to lay on the floor.

Megan Barker (8)
Watton at Stone Primary & Nursery School, Watton at Stone

Tuesday

T errible Tuesday
U nbearable lessons
E qually annoying lunchtime
S eparate lessons
D oomsday Tuesday
A ddition for maths
Y ou should be home by now.

Jake Thomas Millar (10)
Watton at Stone Primary & Nursery School, Watton at Stone

Winter

The icicles dripped over the frozen pond
Clear as glass
The frosted grass
Hidden from sight
Under the snugly snow
The deer and fox
Plodding through the trees.

Amy Rymer (8)
Watton at Stone Primary & Nursery School, Watton at Stone

In The Night

In the night it's dark and spooky
In the night you can't see anything
In the night you go to sleep
In the night things go *bang*
And when things go *bang*
You snuggle into your bed a bit more
And hope for the best.

Joshua Davies (10)
Watton at Stone Primary & Nursery School, Watton at Stone

Friends

F riends are always there to help you out
R unning, jumping and having fun
I n school and out of school, far away or not
E verywhere, you're never alone
N ever do they let you cry, they will always cheer you up
D on't worry, they will never leave you on your own
S o never leave them.

Abbie Phypers (10)
Watton at Stone Primary & Nursery School, Watton at Stone

Dwarves

D o *you* hear creaks in the night?
W ill *you* get kept awake by suspense?
A re *you* going to put up with it anymore?
R ight, that's what I thought
V icious creatures stalking you in the night
E very night you look for one, then you find one
S ee, it was just your dad sneaking downstairs.

James Cunningham (10)
Watton at Stone Primary & Nursery School, Watton at Stone

Pokémon Trip

Dialiga, Palkia and Mew Two
Went to see their mate Pikachu
First they went to Kabuto
But he was in Johto
Then they went to Sinnoh
He is now in Kanto.

Russell Evans (9)
Watton at Stone Primary & Nursery School, Watton at Stone

Who Am I?

I am a supersonic airliner
I do not fly anymore
I used to be the fastest plane around
You'll find me in a museum
I work for British Airways
Who am I?

Matthew Fowler (9)
Watton at Stone Primary & Nursery School, Watton at Stone

Perfect Ref

Football as noisy as the BFG's belly
The crowd whistling, noisy as a hurricane
The dirtiness as the players' attitude thrown onto the ref
The pain affecting the players' game
The chips as horrible as muesli
I would love to be there.

Adam Goold (9)
Watton at Stone Primary & Nursery School, Watton at Stone

War

War is an angry plague that slaughters
And aims lightning at people
War is when iron birds fly over cities
And bomb beautiful homes
War is when giant metal beasts
Trample buildings.

Leo Rolf (11)
Watton at Stone Primary & Nursery School, Watton at Stone

Autumn

A utumn has lots of leaves blustering away
U mbrellas are needed for this type of day
T ODay we can see all the different colours
U ntil the sky turns grey, it starts raining and there's lots of thunder
M ade my umbrella, now it's up in the sky
N ow I'll just have to wait and say goodbye.

Lauren Kelly (10)
Watton at Stone Primary & Nursery School, Watton at Stone

Girls

Girls are great
Girls are the best
They run
And have fun
They play in the sun
Until the day is done.

Zoë Lomas (10)
Watton at Stone Primary & Nursery School, Watton at Stone

Netball

Playing netball, we pass the ball
Playing netball, we shoot and score
Playing netball, they get the ball
Playing netball, they pass the ball
Playing netball, they shoot and score
Playing netball, we draw.

Chloe Marshall (10)
Watton at Stone Primary & Nursery School, Watton at Stone

My World War

Guns shooting, it's disgusting
What we have to put up with
Blowing up buildings
Taking over places like Sherley Castle
But we do it for our country
To save them *we will!*

Ben Cook (8)
Watton at Stone Primary & Nursery School, Watton at Stone

Peace

Peace is the cushion that stops the fists
Peace is the force that keeps friends together
Peace is a creator, not a destroyer
Peace is a life giver, not a life taker
Peace is the medicine, the ointment, the cure
For all those who have been ravaged by war.

Joseph Shepherd (11)
Watton at Stone Primary & Nursery School, Watton at Stone

Animals

Animals, sometimes vicious, sometimes harmless
Sometimes soft, sometimes scruffy
Sometimes cuddly, sometimes shy
Sometimes smelly, sometimes sweet
Sometimes clean, sometimes dirty
Animals, I love mine.

Lauren East (9)
Watton at Stone Primary & Nursery School, Watton at Stone

Cars

Noisy engines
Powerful wheels
Off-roading, dirty
Comfortable seats
Fast gas
Mirrors shine.

Alex Stockley (8)
Watton at Stone Primary & Nursery School, Watton at Stone

War

War is a death-bringer
A ship-sinker
War is a threat to other countries
A bully picking on the weak
When fear comes to stay
That is war.

Max Ellis (11)
Watton at Stone Primary & Nursery School, Watton at Stone

Football

I listen to people shouting out
To give them the ball
Kicking the ball around you
I shoot and I score a goal
One-nil to us.

Amber Daniells (9)
Watton at Stone Primary & Nursery School, Watton at Stone

Horses

Horses gallop
Horses jump over the school
They neigh and neigh
Wander over the farm
They buck and rear in their stable all day.

Kezia Lay (8)
Watton at Stone Primary & Nursery School, Watton at Stone

War

Bombs
Fast, enormous
Exploding, dropping, frightening
Massive explosions everywhere
Devastating.

Joshua Hansing (11)
Watton at Stone Primary & Nursery School, Watton at Stone

Summer

Like a red-hot fireball
Crashes around like a whale
As golden as golden syrup
But still no tail.

Jacob Brett (9)
Watton at Stone Primary & Nursery School, Watton at Stone

Cats

Cats can be big and small
Mine can fit through my door
He cannot fit through the catflap
And his name is Flapjack
Fancy that for a small, fluffy cat.

Arabella Moncur-Byrne (9)
Watton at Stone Primary & Nursery School, Watton at Stone

Hockey

Huffing and puffing
Hitting and shouting
Smelling the sand and the ball
Running and scoring
And feeling the pain of the ball.

Isabel Wing (8)
Watton at Stone Primary & Nursery School, Watton at Stone

Winter

Icicles freezing
Snow so soft
The fluffy white snow
Settles upon the mud and grass
Ready to be a blanket of glittering white.

Megan Sharkey (9)
Watton at Stone Primary & Nursery School, Watton at Stone

Evacuate

Dirty young children
Upset, frightened, it's raining
To the countryside they go
Run away.

James York (10)
Watton at Stone Primary & Nursery School, Watton at Stone

Bombs

Fizzing, spooky
Falling, killing, perishing
Destroying houses, one by one
Weapon.

Raegan Winter-Smith (11)
Watton at Stone Primary & Nursery School, Watton at Stone

Children

Youngsters worried
Waiting, hoping, worrying,
Waiting for the steam train,
Cold.

Oliver Hart (11)
Watton at Stone Primary & Nursery School, Watton at Stone

Apples - Haiku

Apples are very
Crunchy, nice and sweet, nice and
Juicy, good to eat.

Harry Phillips (10)
Watton at Stone Primary & Nursery School, Watton at Stone

Young Writers Information

We hope you have enjoyed reading this book - and that you will continue to enjoy it in the coming years.

If you like reading and writing poetry drop us a line, or give us a call, and we'll send you a free information pack.

Alternatively if you would like to order further copies of this book or any of our other titles, then please give us a call or log onto our website at www.youngwriters.co.uk.

Young Writers Information
Remus House
Coltsfoot Drive
Peterborough
PE2 9JX
(01733) 890066